A Surrey Christmas

A Surrey Christmas

Compiled by John Hudson

SUTTON PUBLISHING

First published in 1996 by
Sutton Publishing Limited · Phoenix Mill
Thrupp · Stroud · Gloucestershire · GL5 2BU

A catalogue record for this book is available from the British Library

ISBN 0-7905-1227-8

Cover picture: Glad Tidings by Spittle (*Photograph: Fine Art Photographs Ltd*)

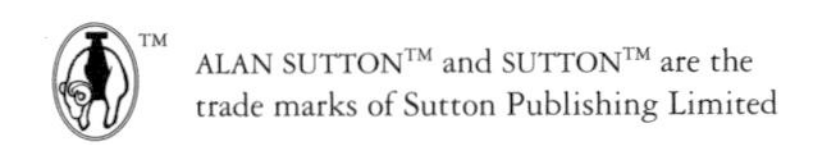

Typeset in Garamond 12/13
Typesetting and origination by
Sutton Publishing Limited
Printed in Great Britain by
Ebenezer Baylis, Worcester.

Contents

Skating on the Thames

When we think of hard weather in Surrey, many of us bring to mind that famous *Illustrated London News* print of 3 March, 1855, showing an impromptu game of ice hockey beside Richmond Bridge. The picture was accompanied in the magazine by only a short account, but one that nevertheless gives us a flavour of the occasion.

It was apparently the first time that the whole width of the river had frozen over at Richmond for seventeen years – in other words, since 1838; the 1830s were a terrible time for biting frosts and deep snow.

Sand was strewn across the river to form paths at two points, one from opposite the Duke of Buccleuch's villa and the other just above the bridge, where the ice was much rougher. Skaters on the Thames, including those immortalized hockey players, were plentiful enough – but the river was too uneven for many, and most skating enthusiasts, 'including a few ladies', preferred the smoother charms of the large ponds in Richmond Park.

Less well known is a set of five drawings of the Thames up-river of London drawn in January, 1891. This again shows a doleful scene at Richmond, plus others at Battersea and Kew, but in these it is more a case of fragmented floating ice rather than solid freezing. There is no doubt that such a scene today would be sensational, as indeed it was in the 1890s, but at

Ice hockey on the river at Richmond, 1855.

Ice floes on the Thames, early 1891.

least it would be credible. One feels that if the river were to freeze solid again, there would be those among us who would think it was the beginning of the end of the world.

While we are supposed to be in a minor ice age now, in the late twentieth century, the effects of global warming are ensuring that we are a long way away from those extraordinary scenes of 1855. A repetition of them would probably leave many of us very frightened indeed – far more so than our allegedly superstitious forefathers, or at least the ice hockey players among them!

Bettesworth's Christmas

GEORGE STURT

George Sturt, or George Bourne to use the pen name by which he was better known in his lifetime, was a novelist and diarist who lived and died in the Farnham area. Two of his most successful volumes, The Bettesworth Book *(1901) and* Memoirs of a Surrey Labourer *(1907) told folksy stories based on conversations with his gardener and handyman Fred Grover when he was living at Vine Cottage in the then hamlet and now Farnham suburb of Lower Bourne. The workman died in 1905, but he also crops up frequently in Sturt's* Journals,

which chronicle the writer's somewhat eventless life. He was cared for by his unmarried sisters, suffered increasingly from strokes and died at his cottage in 1927.

December 27: The weather has remained so wonderfully mild, or 'open', as we say, that outdoor work has received no serious check, and the labouring people were better prepared to face Christmas than it is their wont to be. Bettesworth, amongst others, has had plenty to do, as I have been able to keep him employed.

But looking for him this morning, after the two days' holiday, I discovered him at work in his own part of the garden.

'Oh; going to dig that up this morning?' I asked.

'Ah, it looked so ontidy. An' I ben't jest up to the mark; so I thought I'd have a smack at this.'

Observing him more narrowly, I saw that he looked pale and gently sick. 'Feel a bit Christmassy?' I said.

He looked ashamed, and answered with a feeble smile. 'That is it, sir, to tell ye the truth . . . Some o' my mates with their wives come round to my place last night. They wanted me to goo round to they; but I says "No; I en't goin' out. You best come an' see me". So they all come, an' we made a reg'lar evenin' of it.'

'You've been having a merry Christmas, then?'

'Oh, there's no mistake about that. We did enjoy ourselves. One or two brought a bottle o' home-made wine; an' then there was a jug o' beer, an' so on . . . But I ben't fit for much 's mornin'. I come an' made a start as soon 's 'twas light; but my 'ead was that queer – there 't seemed all mops and brooms. So I says to my ol' gal, "I shall do a bit o' my own today."'

'Perhaps you were up late?'

'Ah, we was. Past the turn o' the night. Turn o' the night? What be I talkin' of? 'Twas two o'clock afore we broke up.'

A handyman and his wife, turn of the century.

(Remember that during the winter Bettesworth is generally in bed by half-past eight or nine o'clock). 'An' we did git merry, too. Got to singin' at last.'

'Oh! You did go it. We were pretty quiet, up here.'

'Well, there didn't seem to be nothin' gwine on nowhere. I come out once while they was singin'. An' all up the valley was as quiety . . . There didn't seem to be nobody about, an' nothin' gwine on nowheres, 'xcept 'twas at my place. But I heerd ol' Biggs – my neighbour, ye know – sayin', "What! Bettesworth's got a party of 'em, then! That's the fust time since we bin here." An' when I went indoors agen, I says to 'em, "You be disturbin' the neighbours." But we did enjoy ourselves, an' no mistake.'

I tried to imagine the jolly party: eight of them in a little stuffy room, with a paraffin lamp and the reek of tobacco smoke to aid the fire in keeping them warm. Want of ventilation had probably more than the beer and wine to do with the old man's headache. Besides, he had had too little sleep.

'I don't wonder,' I said, 'that you feel queer, if you didn't get to bed before two o'clock.'

''Twas purty well three afore I got to bed . . . And then I got up . . . Well, the clock struck six, and my ol' gal she says, "There's six o'clock. Ben't ye goin' to git up?" "No," I says, "I shall have another half-hour." I wa'n't ready to turn out. An' there I laid, ontil the clock warned for seven. Then I did git out an' lit the fire. But I ses to the old gal, "My head do ache," I says. "So do mine," she says.'

The old man seemed needlessly cast down and ashamed. I tried to encourage him, and suggested that 'it'll wear off as the day goes on'.

'Oh, yes, sir! It'll wear off. Now I be about – there, I seems better a'ready. 'Twas jest at first startin' I seemed so queer. But once I can git on workin' and git into a good sweat I shall do.'

And his surmise was correct. Before night came round again, all his discomfort had vanished; and the pleasant recollections of his cheerful evening remained unsullied.

The Singing Men

JOHN MOORE

In truth this is not a Christmas recollection, but it captures the spirit of a Surrey country pub in the inter-war years as well as any writing I know, and it certainly captures the spirit of John Moore. He was the writer whose Brensham Trilogy of rural life books immortalized his native Tewkesbury in Gloucestershire and its surrounding countryside and although the three books are scarcely fashionable now, they have been successfully televised in recent years. Moore came from a long line of country auctioneers, and prided himself on his ready rapport with all sorts and conditions of men. Perhaps the main problem with reading his work today is not that it does not ring true of his time, but the extent to which life has moved on since then. While reading this account of half-a-dozen men singing uproariously in a pub for hours on end, from his 1939 book A Walk Through Surrey, *I confess that I find it hard to let my thoughts and sympathies stray from some imagined couple in the corner who had just come out for a quiet drink.*

Just as this was the best day's walking, so was it also the best evening after walking.

I got to Holmbury St Mary at about half-past five and when I had had a look at its very lovely modern church I went to the pub, where I immediately fell in with five remarkable men with whom I spent the rest of the day.

George was a very fat man with a beetroot-coloured face and the pleasant leer of some wicked idol. Willie was a tall, thin sardonic fellow with only one arm, who looked rather like a pirate. Perce was a stolid youth with the hands and battered ears of a boxer. Eric, the youngest of the five, was a tow-headed giant who spoke little and drank much. And the one they called Matt had close-cropped hair and wore the appearance of one who had but recently come out of prison.

I do not know whether this comic-opera crew belonged to Holmbury St Mary, or whether they were merely staying there. In fact I know hardly anything about them, although I spent four hours in their company, because for at least three of those hours we were singing. Lord, how we sang!

George may have looked like a debased Buddha, Willie like Captain Hook, Perce like a bruiser from a travelling fair, and Matt like a convict, while Eric may have been – indeed Eric was – considerably drunk. But one and all they had splendid voices, one and all they loved singing and they knew the right songs.

I cannot remember how the singing started; I am inclined to think that they were already singing when I entered the bar at half-past six. We had an interval for supper – a country-pub supper of bread-and-cheese and onions and pickled walnuts – at about eight, and after that we sang till closing time. We sang as men should sing in a pub, with beer mugs in our hands; whenever we stopped singing we drank, and sang the lustier for it when we began again. If there was a chorus we roared it, and made everybody in the bar join in; and when

The Red Cross Inn and Slip Shoe Street, Reigate, 1906.

the chorus was ended, Eric, whose speech during the latter part of the evening was confined to one strange expletive, would say, appreciatively, 'Coolumme-days!' and sink his pint manfully. Then while more drinks were fetched by the barmaid we would begin as if by common consent to sing another song.

And that was a curious thing. I do not remember any one of us, at any time during the evening, actually suggesting a song. Nobody said 'Let's sing Spanish Ladies'; but we suddenly started singing Spanish Ladies as if we had rehearsed it.

Nobody said: 'I wonder if we all know Greensleeves'; we simply began to sing Greensleeves, all together. There was no popular song in English or French unknown to the Singing Men of Holmbury St Mary.

We began with the shanties. We sang 'In Amsterdam there dwelt a Maid', and 'Rio', of course, and:

> Early in the morning
> A sailor likes the lassies, O!

And 'Sally Brown' (which is perhaps the best tune of them all), and 'Shenandoah' and 'Hanging Johnnie':

> They call me Hanging Johnnie
> Away-ay-i-o.
> They sez I hangs for money,
> So hang, boys, hang.

And the 'Drunken Sailor' and 'Blow the Man Down' and 'Whiskey is the Life of Man' and 'Johnny Gone to Hilo' and a dozen more. Then for a change we sang some ballads, 'Widdecombe Fair' and 'Ilkla Moor' and of course 'Billy Boy' with its lovely last verse:

> Did she lie close unto thee, Billy Boy, Billy Boy?
> Did she lie close unto thee, Billy Boy?
> Yes, she lay close unto me
> As the bark is to the tree,
> And me Nancy kittled me fancy, oh me charming
> Billy Boy!

Next we sang Scottish songs, 'Speed Little Boat' and 'Weel May the Keel Row' and 'Green Grow the Rushes, O!' and

> The bonnie Earl of Moray
> He was the Queen's luve!

We ransacked the world for songs to sing. We stole 'Men of

Harlech' from Wales and 'The Shan Wan Wocht' from Ireland and 'Aupres de ma Blonde' from France and 'I Got a Robe' from Louisiana and 'Frankie and Johnnie' from New York. We sandwiched drinking songs between 'Mistress Mine' and 'Come Away Death', and 'John Peel' between war songs like 'Tipperary' and 'Mademoiselle from Armentieres'. We sang till the sweat stood out on our foreheads and George's beetroot-coloured face went deep purple, and between singing we still drank, and Eric, sublimely happy, said, 'Coolumme-days!' because it was all he could say.

By closing-time we hadn't nearly sung ourselves out: we still had a score of songs as it were on the tip of our tongues to sing; and I thought how rich and wonderful the English language was, how inexhaustible, how generous, how prodigal, for we had been singing from six till ten, we had

Time passing slowly at Abinger Hammer.

never sung the same song twice, and we could easily have sung for another four hours before we need resort to the slick, cheap trivialities of Gilbert and Sullivan! I said something of the kind, rather incoherently, to Eric, but he only stared at me happily and murmured: 'Coolumme-days!'

Then the barmaid said 'Time, gentlemen, please!' and we begged 'Just one more song before we go!' so she grinned and said: 'Well, make it a clean one in case the bobby's outside', and we tried to blow the roof off with 'Daisy'. Then we shook hands all round, and I went to the door and saw them off, and I thought that in the dusk they looked the most fearful cut-throat crew imaginable, and yet I loved them all.

'Good night!' they cried. 'Good night!' I echoed, hating to see them go.

'Coolumme-days!' said Eric, speaking like a man in a dream.

Christmas and the Customer

Pack up your troubles in your old kit bag and shop, shop, shop. That seems to be the message of the Richmond & Twickenham Home Journal *of January 1915, looking back on the first Christmas of the Great War. By now even the poor*

displaced Belgians have been transformed into yet more customers for the Richmond shops, not to mention the war-torn soldiers and sailors at the home recently converted for them from the once mighty Star and Garter Hotel on Richmond Hill. The mobilization of the nurseries of Richmond, reported without comment, seems particularly chilling. Even on a miniature scale, it seems, the right of arms dealers to make a killing in more ways than one seems to be a liberty to be fought for and prized.

The darkest of clouds has a silver lining. Christmas at Richmond bears testimony to the truth of this adage. Here and there in the borough are homes which have suffered grievous blows from which they will never recover, and in many others the festivities have been tempered with keen anxiety for the safety and comfort of those at the front. But

Every nursery mobilized, Richmond, Christmas, 1914.

from a purely business point of view, Richmond has had little to grumble at, and much to be thankful for. The streets have been as crowded as ever, not only with residents but with those who live in the neighbourhood and who always regard Richmond as their shopping centre.

Seldom has trade been so brisk. Although our thoroughfares have been as dark and cheerless as Berlin could wish, the inhabitants were inside the shops, not lying trembling abed. The persistent rain which washed our pavements just before Christmas aided the absence of gaslight in defeating the labours of the window dresser, but both afflictions merely sent people into the shops as purchasers instead of remaining outside as spectators. Moreover, a great deal of the War Loan and other abnormal national expenditure has been spent in the town. The Red Cross Hospital is a good consumer of commodities; the Belgian refugees are spending in the borough the funds which the burgesses have raised for their relief, and the thousand hefty lads at the Star and Garter Barracks have bought little presents for the two thousand girls they left behind them, to say nothing of those whom they met here.

One interesting feature in the Christmas shopping has been the extraordinary demand for toy soldiers and weapons. All the nurseries of Richmond have mobilized, and each little Kitchener is insistent in the demands he makes upon his parents for 'more men and yet more'.

Lighting the Dorking Lamps

CHARLES ROSE

In his Recollections of Old Dorking, *published by the* West Surrey Times *in 1878, Charles Rose looked back half a century, to before Victoria's reign. He often notes in his dialogue that certain events and customs have not changed, but they all seem a world away to us today. In this first excerpt from his book, he talks us through just another day in the Dorking of his youth; muffin sellers, lamplighters, mail coach men and all.*

Let us pay an imaginary visit to the town half a century ago, this time on a winter's day. We see in the streets elderly matrons with scarlet cloaks, large black bonnets lined with white, and large bordered caps extending to below the chin. There are maidens also attired in short-waisted dresses, beaver bonnets and cloaks of a similar shape to those of their seniors. The men we meet, too, are dressed in clothes of an old-fashioned cut. Among the elders of the middle class are to be seen ancient greatcoats, knee breeches and top boots; among the juniors and middle-aged of the same class, pigeon-tailed, broad-collared, gilt-buttoned dress coats, and frilled shirt fronts; while among the sturdy sons of toil, dark round frocks, rough beaver hats and high leather leggings are the general favourites.

Horse trough, horseless carriages, White Horse Hotel, Dorking.

Let us gratify our curiosity by learning the price of provisions. We enter a grocer's shop and find the rates of foreign produce to be very high. Tea, a mixture of Congou and Twankay, the quality generally drunk, is eight shillings the pound. The best kinds of tea, gunpowder and Pekoe, are from twelve to fifteen shillings; moist sugar in ordinary use is eight pence, lump sugar a shilling, best loaf 1*s* 2*d*, and in the summer it is eleven pence. Prime bacon 7½*d*, Derby and double Gloucester cheese eight pence, Cheshire nine pence per pound. Salt, chiefly in consequence of duty, is 5½*d* per pound. We find at the butcher's that prime joints of beef are 8½*d* per pound, mutton seven pence. The pork butcher is selling fresh pork, legs, spare ribs and griskins, at 6½*d*, while those with little cash – from the low rate of wages and the number of mouths to feed – can buy the 'hands' at five pence per pound.

EPSOM AND EWELL
LITERARY AND SCIENTIFIC INSTITUTION.

The Fifth of a Second Series of

READINGS

WILL BE GIVEN

On WEDNESDAY, 10th DECEMBER, 1862,

IN THE LECTURE ROOM OF THE INSTITUTION.

SUBJECT	AUTHOR	READER.
Rural Life in England ..	Irving	Mr. J. Harrowell, Jun.
Rather hard to take	Anon	Mr. F. Marfleet.
The Broken Crutch	Bloomfield ..	Rev. J. Donovan, B.A.
The One Legged Goose .	Anon	Mr. J. Andrews.
Story of Le Fevre	Sterne	Mr. Murrell.
Doingsat DotheBoys Hall	Dickens .. .	Mr. S. Marfleet.

Doors open at ¼ to 8 o'Clock, Reading to commence at ¼ past 8 PRECISELY.
Admission :—THREEPENCE. Members FREE.

Gentlemen willing to assist in the Readings will much OBLIGE by forwarding their Names and Subjects (which should not occupy more than ten to fifteen minutes in the reading) to the Secretary at their earliest convenience.

☞ **THESE READINGS ARE GIVEN EVERY ALTERNATE WEDNESDAY.**

Andrews, Printer, High Street, Epsom.

The small town social scene: a Christmas reading at the Epsom and Ewell Literary and Scientific Institution – the 'Lit and Sci' – in 1862. The anonymous tale 'The One Legged Goose' looks as if it might have had a seasonal flavour, while as usual the superstar Dickens is represented with 'Doings at Dotheboys Hall'.

The afternoon arrives, and we hear the cheery cry of 'Master' Woodger, the muffin and crumpet vendor, the stall keeper and delighter of the juveniles at Dorking and Punchbowl fairs – 'Muffins O! Crumpets O! Crumpets too!' The shades of evening are coming on, and we peer into the doorway of one of the smaller shops. The proprietor is stooping intently and patiently over a little round box on the counter before him. He is obtaining a light with flint and steel, tinder and brimstone match, for the more convenient and quickly lighting lucifer was not then invented. He now lights here and there a candle, and thus poorly illuminated, the little establishment is kept open till nine or maybe ten o'clock. The larger establishments are better lighted – not, however, by gas, for which Dorking had to wait a little while longer, but by the old lamp then in vogue.

We now see in the distance a wooden-legged man hastening along, and at his heels and on either side are a number of small boys. He approaches, torch in hand, and with ladder on his shoulder, the nearest lamp in his way. This is lamplighter Wicks, who during the day has trimmed and stocked with oil the lamp he has now come to light. He climbs the ladder with marvellous rapidity, and the work of lighting over, descends with a slide. Then, amid a shout of the juveniles, he starts off to the next lamp, cracking jokes with the boys, and now and then saluting them with a blow of his wooden leg. The ringers, in the course of the evening, are at their wonted practice, and the bells give forth a merry peal. Otherwise, however, there is but little to interest, and little to cheer in the dimly-lighted streets.

The hours pass on, and nine o'clock arrives. Soon after this, the mail cart stops at the post office, opposite the Wheatsheaf Inn. The mailman, well coated and muffled, at once withdraws his horse pistols from the holsters, proves to the acting official that they are duly loaded and returns to the cart

to place them whence they were taken. He now waits outside for the mail bags, and while doing so, sundry and divers movements are afoot, indicating to the passer-by that the mailman is a penny the richer for a too late, yet important, letter. The sealing of the bags is at length completed, and they are now deposited in the cart in safety. This accomplished, the mailman is quickly seated on his narrow box, and off he starts for Kingston, to return in the small hours of the morning. Such, in mere outline, were the appearance, life and usages of old Dorking. In some respects, at least, its present inhabitants have but little cause to wish for a return of the 'good old times'.

Christmas Stocking

JANET HILLS

Janet Hills, a film and television critic for The Times *and its Educational Supplement, died at the age of 36 in 1956. She was born in Epsom in 1919, the daughter of a doctor, but was brought up in the West Country after her family had moved to Gloucestershire. Bright and sparky, she would clearly have made her mark in the media world, and perhaps as a creative writer. There is certainly verve enough in this story, found in a collection titled* Fragments, *published by her grieving family not long after her death.*

Before I give myself over to Christmas good will, I am making a list of the people whom I would like to murder. Every day I collect a few more, and I am knitting their descriptions into a huge purple stocking. I do not know any of their names.

Bypassing milk bottles and cats, I shall go straight to the first human beings who upset my day. At 8.35 a.m. they are waiting for me in the Underground, pressed against the fivepenny ticket machine while they search all their pockets for money. When I have finally dislodged them and put in my sixpence, they lean over my shoulder and insert another so that our change is mingled. By this ruse they beat me to the escalator, where they stand on the left side entertaining their friends, with their elbows sticking out like branches.

In the train they do not quite manage to get seats because rows of sturdy young men in city black are there already, entrenched behind newspapers; but they sweep the weaker passengers away from the straps and the walls. Then they light cigarettes and gesture with them as they talk, thus distracting attention from their sharp-edged suitcases which lie in wait in the middle of the floor. At Paddington, thank goodness, some of them get out and set off to besiege the booking office with detailed questions about times and platforms of trains, while a queue forms and the enquiry office stands empty. Jostling their way to the doors, they ostentatiously trip over my carefully arranged briefcase and bag, and glance at me reproachfully.

Out in the open air again, I wait at the bus stop, mentally working on my stocking. Here the tactics vary. Sometimes my enemies rush past me on the gutter side while I am waiting for my turn to get on, and snarl because I am in their way. At other times, still more diabolically, they stand in front of me, stolidly staring at the bus until I try to pass them, when they

become indignantly obstructive. Inside, they refuse to pass along the car and the conductor will not let me travel on the step, so I have to stand on one foot all the way. On the other hand, if by any chance the bus happens to be almost empty, they ignore vacant seats and sink down beside me, breathing heavily and propping parcels against my legs. I am a tolerant person, and I have no objection to passengers who do plain knitting; but cable stitch, with its third needle, is simply aggressive, and people ought to wait till they get home before they turn the heels of socks.

At lunchtime, when I make my harmless way to Oxford Street, my enemies are there, too, walking four abreast with linked arms or plunging headlong out of side streets. Without any warning they stop dead and stare into windows, then glance sideways gloatingly as I pull up with such skilled swiftness that someone runs into me from behind. When I am in a hurry they move as slowly as treacle from a spoon; but if at last I decide to turn sideways into a shop, they thunder forwards and sweep me off my course, baring their teeth and prodding with umbrellas. I cannot buy a toy unmolested. One of them has got there first, and is asking how all the different brick games work and explaining the tastes of his seven youngest children. As my turn comes, another sidles up and calls over my shoulder: 'Might I just ask a question?' and then, without waiting for an answer, launches into a complaint and has to be led off to the manager. Someone else stands by to buttonhole the assistant on his way back, and no one else will serve me as bricks are very specialized.

The only thing left to me is to eat – and in all the cafés I can see my enemies hunched over 1,000-page novels while they flick cigarette ash into empty coffee cups. So in the end I go to a place with trays and there, just in front of me, is a familiar figure who changes his mind three times as to

which is the largest helping of stewed gooseberries and, grabbing backwards, slops my coffee into the saucer while his sleeve brushes through the artificial cream. Meanwhile, rather too close behind me, another one makes clucking noises and shoves with her tray, simply because I am exercising my right as an Englishwoman to make up my mind in my own time.

At the end of the day, of course, the persecutions of travel are reversed; but a new one is added, for I have bought an evening paper, a luxury which my enemies apparently cannot afford. So they all look over my shoulder or stare at the back, and seem quite affronted when I turn a page. Yesterday, being for once paperless, I discovered yet another kind of aggression, for when I happened to glance absent-mindedly at a *Star* just in front, its owner turned round pointedly and spread it out under my eyes – so that I was forced to gaze out of the window for the entire bus ride.

I almost forgot to mention that at the top of my stocking I am knitting a special rib for the income tax authorities. Since, however, I believe in scrupulous justice, I have not yet decided on the exact design – for I am waiting to discover whether it is really the Inspector of Taxes (4th floor, 'D') or the Collector of Taxes (London, 16th Collection, Entrance 'B') who must be held responsible for the demand so lovingly saved up and timed with such deadly accuracy for the day when I made my first Christmas shopping list.

Nice as Pie

What's in a name? Nothing very appetizing, it seems, when it comes to the small community of Christmaspie, near Woking. Was this the scene of some gargantuan feast, the baking of the greatest pie in the whole wintry world? Arthur Bonner and his colleagues who published *The Place Names of Surrey* in 1934 certainly do not think so. They note that a Thomas Christmas was recorded in a parish register of 1575, and a John Christmas in 1619, and surmise that there might be a connection. There was certainly a Christmas Pie Farm here in 1823, and if you had a name like that, you might well want to have a little fun with it when it came to naming your property.

As the phone book will tell you, the fact is that in Surrey, 'Christmas' is by no means an unusual surname, and this has been the case for centuries. It crops up in parish records across the county, and Bonner's 1934 place names book unearthed its use in two other rural spots in the sixteenth century – Christmas Farm, near Reigate, in 1598 and Christmas Hill or Hills in 1553.

Christmas sports.

Gifts for Tiny Tims

The Castelnau Church Monthly, *attached to Holy Trinity Church at Barnes, mixed religious teaching with a strong social conscience. In this January excerpt, looking back on Christmas 1895, a vivid picture is painted of the rush of seasonal activity at the great Harrods' depository beside the Thames at Barnes. Talk of a cripples' fund bringing help to the Tiny Tims of London makes us squirm today, but we must remind ourselves that even fifty years ago such sentiments would have seemed unexceptionable to most people.*

Christmas has again come and gone. With ourselves, the season this year has been of a quiet and uneventful character. The Church was very handsomely decorated, and the Choir, though somewhat attenuated by the Christmas vacation, did its part ably. The thanks of the congregation are certainly due to those who with willing hearts and ready hands have thus helped by their gifts, or their services.

In the relief of the poor, usual at this season, the ordinary almsgiving of the Church was considerably extended, as well as supplemented by a supply of Barnes Christmas Gifts. Garments for old and young have been freely distributed, these being the gifts of the Castelnau Working Party, the Castelnau Sewing Circle, the South-west London College Needlework Guild and the Surrey Needlework Guild. We rejoice to find that the spirit of Dorcas still survives amongst us.

Besides those benefited by our own Christmas gifts, four of our

Feeding poor boys at a soup kitchen.

young parishioners were the glad recipients of the generous bounty of the *Daily Telegraph* Cripples' Christmas Dinner Fund, consisting for each of a large amply filled hamper of provisions and a sack of coals. It seemed only fitting that some of this unique and liberal charity should be bestowed in our own neighbourhood, wherein nearly all the several thousand hampers were packed for delivery. It was a great and imposing sight to see the long array of well-horsed vans heavily packed with their full hampers, all moving together from Harrods' Stores Depository to carry good cheer and gladness for Christmas-tide to the homes of all the 'Tiny Tims' of the Metropolis; a sight also that bore witness at once to the power of the press, the charity of the great public heart, and to the enterprise, energy, and resources of our modern commercial world.

Short Truce in a Desperate Christmas

BOB OGLEY

The year 1940 was the low point of the war for many Britons. German bombs were pounding our towns, cities and stray country communities, too, and at this point there was no sound reason to believe that at the end of it all we would come out victorious. Here Bob Ogley recreates the scene in an extract from his recent book Surrey at War. *The fires were blazing in London, the emergency services were stretched to their limit; but at least people still found time to pack the Kingston Empire's panto – and grumble about income tax, a bogy that would be with us long after we had seen off Mr Hitler.*

Christmas, 1940 was the most desperate that Surrey had ever faced – but as with beleaguered people all over England, the citizens gritted their teeth, took their Horlicks, cleared away the debris and carried on.

The county newspapers were of one accord in noting that this was a very sad Yuletide. The editor of the *Surrey Advertiser* wrote: 'While maintaining the formal atmosphere of the festival as fully as possible, it has been impossible to forget

those who have gone to the wars. Into many homes thousands of men and women on service have been welcomed and thousands of others, driven from their homes by tragic experience or danger, have been remembered.'

Looking ahead, he said: 'As the New Year approaches, we welcome the lengthening of the light. We have left the shortest day behind and the sun begins to climb in the heavens. It is a happy augury that the moral blackout is fading, too. The shortest day for the oppressed peoples of Europe is past. Daily, fresh evidence comes that the enslaved nations are stirring in the darkness.'

In Surrey, then, people did their best to observe the traditions of the season. The Kingston Empire was fully booked for its production of Mother Goose, starring Joe Arthur. The London Philharmonic Orchestra, all seventy of them, were pulling in the customers to the Rembrandt, Ewell. The Hogs Back Hotel was advertizing a special Christmas Day lunch for six shillings and a dinner-dance on Christmas Eve for 12*s* 6*d*.

There was no let-up in money-raising activities, and the desire to help touched young and old. A feature of Camberley School's bazaar in the school hall was an attractive display of knitted garments by the girls, the fund to be directed to 'the relief of distress caused by enemy action'. Ewhurst organized a 'delightful Christmas programme of events', including an auction conducted by Richard Gouldon; Mr Penny of BBC fame. Ten pounds was raised in aid of comforts for the village Home Guard.

Many people found the bottle a welcome distraction from the bombs, and during the Christmas week the newspapers reported several cases of drunkenness. Fourteen people were summoned at Guildford for failing to comply with light regulations, and four cyclists for riding without screened and dimmed red rear lights.

One happier story came from Farnham, where the little Playhouse Theatre, now the Redgrave, was almost a year old and was putting on some fine performances. The timber-framed building had been put to many uses in the past as a warehouse, cloth factory, roller-skating rink and music school. During 1940 it was turned into a small theatre with tip-up seats and a raked auditorium that could hold 167 people at 1*s* 6*d* and 3*s* 6*d*. By Christmas 1940 it was one of the country's smallest reps, opening with Shaw's *You Never Can Tell*.

There was an undeclared amnesty during the Christmas period, but this ended with a vengeance on December 29–30 when the enemy attempted to burn down the City of London, and nearly succeeded. Firemen from all over Surrey rushed to help, and probably there had never been such a concentration of fire fighters and equipment brought into action at one time. Certainly Croydon sent a large contingent under Chief Officer Delve. The fires from London were enormous and visible from scores of miles from all sides; it seemed to the people of Surrey, and particularly to those living on higher ground, that the whole of London was being consumed.

As the great fires of London raged, newspapers were full of pleas for help. Esher was seriously short of wardens. Epsom and Ewell wanted volunteers for stretcher parties and demolition work. Sutton needed women for first aid posts and auxiliary nursing, while every community called for more recruits to the Home Guard. Only Malden, it seemed, was satisfied. There, the Civil Defence boasted that all its machinery was in place and ready for maximum operation.

There were many people experiencing an English Christmas for the first time, and among them were more than 600 Belgian and Dutch refugees who had found a safe haven in Surrey homes after a 'second trek from German barbarism'. The refugees had arrived at Wimbledon station earlier in the year with terrible stories of Nazi atrocities. They were met by the WVS, who found

them homes in Kingston, Wimbledon, Surbiton and Esher, Hook and other towns in the north of the county.

In these hours of darkness there were some lighter moments – as a letter written in 1940 and discovered in Elmbridge Museum, Weybridge more than fifty years later, clearly shows. It was written by Mr A. Citizen, Flattened Road, Much Blasted, Surrey and was addressed to HM Collector of Taxes. It read: 'For the following reasons I am unable to meet your demands for Income Tax. I have been bombed, blasted, burnt, sandbagged, walked upon, sat upon, held up, held down, flattened out and squeezed by Income Tax, Super Tax, Tobacco Tax, Purchase Tax, Beer Tax, Spirit Tax, Motor Tax, Entertainment Tax and every society, organization and club that the inventive mind of man can conceive to extract what I may or may not have in my possession for the Red Cross, Black Cross, Double Cross and every other cross and hospital in the town.'

Deep and Crisp and Even

Good King Wenceslas, a favourite with carol singers for generations, was written by a novelist and lyricist with Shepperton close to his heart. John Mason Neale was born in

1818 and died just forty-eight years later, but in his short life he found time to make the community famous in his day in *Shepperton Manor*; a tale of religious unrest set in the seventeenth century; and in the bold, stirring *Wenceslas* he produced a piece that will be sung as long as joyous voices celebrate the season of Christmas.

At times, the dialogue of the Shepperton novel echoes the slightly unreal conversation between Wenceslas and his page:

> The wind roared round the thatched eaves of the Swan at Chertsey and the rain was pouring in torrents when the two travellers rode up, drenched to the skin. . . "How far is it to Shepperton?" asked one. . . "To Shepperton?" cried the hostler. "Your worships may rest content that no mortal man could get to Shepperton on such a night as this. . ."

A glide and a fall.

Perhaps Neale was no great novelist, but he shone as a writer and translator of hymns. As well as *Good King Wenceslas*, he gave the world such enduring classics as *Jerusalem the Golden* and *O Happy Band of Pilgrims*, and counted *All Glory, Laud and Honour* and *O Come, O Come Emmanuel* among his scores of translations. Maybe he was influenced in his beliefs by the long-serving Rector of Shepperton, the Reverend William Russell, who taught him from 1823 to 1829, when he was living in the village with his mother and three sisters after his father's death. Whatever, he was a frequent visitor to the Rectory for the rest of his life, working away at worthy church histories in between the flashes of inspiration in which he produced words to reach to the very heart of Christmas and Christianity.

Wassailing the Apple Tree

E.W. SWANTON

Working just before the First World War, Swanton rummaged around the written and spoken history of his neighbourhood to produce Bygone Haslemere. *As is the case with many a local*

historian, he is most entertaining when he lets his hair down in the folkore and customs chapter, and those magical phrases 'it is said' and 'the story goes' are rightly allowed to cover a multitude of factual sins. He did not have too much to say about Christmas, but what he did give us was a Surrey version of the widespread wassailing tradition.

Some inhabitants of Haslemere remember the ceremony of wassailing the apple trees at Anstead Brook on New Year's Eve. The wassailers met in the orchard, stood around a favourite tree, rapped it with sticks, and shouted:

> Here stands a good old apple tree, stand fast root.
> Every little twig bear an apple big,
> Hats full, caps full and three score sacks full.
> Hip! hip!! hurrah!!!"

A loud blast, three times repeated, was then blown at the base of the tree.

Christmas greetings from the Jameses of Glenfield, Esher, 1910.

After the performance had been repeated at a few other trees, the company adjourned to the farmhouse where, we are told, the farmer gave them elderberry wine, cake and small coin. The wine must have been an innovation, for the correct wassail drink of two centuries ago was ale, with roasted apples, sugar, nutmeg and toast in it.

Spirited Little Girl

FRANCES D. STEWART

Elsewhere in this book, the Surrey writer George Bourne asks why we should be so preoccupied with ghost stories at Christmas. Good question, especially since the Bethlehem story is more supernatural than anything you will ever hear elsewhere. Perhaps the answer lies in our age-old delight of scaring one another with fireside tales on winter's evenings. How I dreaded, on such nights, to leave the cheerful company to dash to the bathroom through the still, cold, silent house beyond the sitting room door. My excuse for using these stories, and others by Frances Stewart elsewhere in the book, is that they all have Christmas connections. These come from Surrey Ghosts Old and New, *published in 1990.*

Some time ago a police officer living in Norwood had a lot of 'aggravation' from a little girl about ten to twelve years old.

He was probably the right person to deal with a mischievous child, you might think, but it is a difficult task when she is from another age and comes and goes as she pleases.

The first time he saw her it was about midday and she was standing in the rear bedroom window of his house. Dressed in Victorian costume, her black boots polished to perfection, she watched, perhaps enviously, as the children of Sylvan High School romped in the playground below.

Soon after this he awoke one morning after his wife and son had left the house, and walked along to the bathroom. As he opened the door he was surprised to find jewellery which had been in the rear bedroom strewn across the bathroom floor. He returned the jewellery to its correct place, and then went to the kitchen. Later, he returned to the bathroom, only to discover that the floor was once again littered with the coloured trinkets. Angrily, he went into the hall and shouted: 'Please leave the jewellery alone!' He then heard a scraping noise, and turning quickly, saw his tool boxes slide from their shelf and crash to the floor as if pushed by an unseen hand. He examined the shelf closely, but it was perfectly level and as firmly fixed as before.

There were no further disturbances, and he began to forget the incidents until Christmas Eve. He went out for a few drinks with some colleagues and invited them back to the house for a nightcap. As they were leaving, three of them had gone into the street but the fourth remained at the bottom of the stairs. They could hear he was talking, and when they asked him what he was up to he said he had been asking the little girl why she wasn't in bed. They all turned to look back, but she had gone.

When researching ghosts one must learn to expect the unexpected, but I was most unprepared for the following story from a family living on the outskirts of Croydon. For some years they had owned a spaniel dog. He was not friendly

to strangers and quite possessive towards his owners, but they loved him just the same. Eventually he had to be put to sleep, and the family missed him so much that it was not long before they had a replacement in the form of a young labrador. Unlike the previous dog, he loved everyone and was into everything. At Christmas his enthusiasm knew no bounds, and the lady owner took some photographs of him as he 'helped' his master unwrap a suitcase that had been given to him.

Some time later the film was developed, with amazing results. In the first picture the man was kneeling on the floor, the dog beside him intent on the parcel. In the second the animal seems to have been slightly distracted, and a small shadow is appearing in the right hand corner. In the third picture, however, the dog is leaning backwards as if to avoid something, his fur is ruffled and he stares wide-eyed to the right. The grey shadow has become the distinct shape of a spaniel with long floppy ears, and his nose is almost touching that of the labrador. A photograph of the previous dog showed it exactly to resemble the phantom. Was it jealousy that made the old rascal return?

A family living in a council house in Thornton Heath in the 1970s would be the first to agree that hauntings are not confined to old buildings. Their first startling experience was in August 1972 when they were woken in the middle of the night by their bedside radio playing classical music at full volume. As the husband pressed down the button to stop the noise he noticed it was tuned to a foreign programme, and not as he had set it on retiring. Apart from a lampshade that developed the habit of leaping to the floor, nothing else happened until Christmas.

As the husband was sweeping the living room floor a Christmas decoration hurled itself across the room and hit his head as if it had been aimed deliberately. As he sat down to

recover the Christmas tree began to shake violently and he was showered with its needles.

With the New Year the ghost's activities began in earnest. Footsteps would be heard in the bedroom when nobody was there, and one night the son woke to find what he described as a man in old fashioned dress standing at the foot of his bed. The figure stared at him menacingly before vanishing.

On another occasion the family were entertaining friends when at about 12.30 a.m. there was loud knocking at the front door; then the living room door flew open, and all the house lights came on at once. Such disturbances continued to cause so much irritation that in 1974 they had the house blessed.

Living Memories

In the early 1990s the County Federation of Women's Institutes compiled Surrey Within Living Memory, *drawing upon its members' recollections. Needless to say, there was no shortage of material when the Christmas section came along. . . .*

Once or twice when I was very small in the 1920s, I was woken early on Christmas morning by carols being sung outside our house at Kenley by the choir of the Salvation Army. It was very dark, as it was only about two o'clock. I can still hear the magical sounds of 'Hark, the Herald Angels Sing' floating through the

Guildford High Street, scene of Christmas shopping expeditions without number.

still night air, and of course I crept out of bed to feel the bulging stocking hanging on the bedpost. Father Christmas and the beautiful singing – my heart was just bursting.

* * *

Once a year before Christmas in the 1920s, the Revd Mr Grundy arranged a parochial tea in Chobham village hall. This cost sixpence, and there would be readings from Dickens. Just before Christmas a pig would be killed and hung up outside the shop of Lascelles, opposite the church. On the appointed evening flares lit up the scene, and folk paid sixpence to guess the pig's weight. The winners had vouchers to be cashed in the shop; needless to say, the local farmers were often the lucky ones.

* * *

A truly exciting memory is of lighting the Christmas tree with candles, which burned with a flickering light in the metal holders clipped on to the branches.

* * *

At Christmas in the 1930s the grocer's window was transformed into an Aladdin's cave. The shop window was beautifully set out, not months ahead but early in December, with boxes of crackers edged with glitter, and some of them with little celluloid dolls on the front. Baskets of crystallized fruits, jars of stem ginger and round boxes of Chinese figs. Marzipan fruits, glistening piles of shiny unstoned raisins and tall glass jars of sugared almonds. Large York hams, jars of game in aspic and Gentleman's Relish with hunting scenes painted on the pottery lids. Families had fairly plain and wholesome food most of the time. The Christmas feast, therefore, was very special – and not surprizingly, often ended in tears, or worse, for the younger members of the family – and some of the older ones, too!

Christmas Day was magical. The tree was always dressed on Christmas Eve, after the children had been put to bed. We went downstairs on Christmas morning to see the lighted tree for the first time. My mother always expected to have at least a dozen people round the table at lunchtime, to be joined by another dozen or so assorted aunts, uncles, cousins and friends for tea and the rest of the day. The preparation involved must have been awesome, despite the many pairs of willing hands.

We always played party games between teatime and supper – Chinese Whispers, Postman's Knock, Charades, Pass the Parcel, Consequences . . . Two things made Christmas Day complete. First, when supper was cleared away – how did we tuck away yet another meal? – we played hilarious card games when everybody cheated; Chase the Ace and Newmarket. A

halfpenny on the cards and a penny in the kitty! The thrill if you won at the end, when all the money was piled on to one card. The other special happening was the whole family round the piano singing carols and favourite songs. My father and his elder brother led the singing, with another brother playing the piano; their *pièce de résistance* was 'Just a Song at Twilight'. It brings a lump to my throat to hear it now, and memories of many happy Christmases – and a very happy and secure childhood – come flooding back.

* * *

Grandmama was less than five feet tall but she ruled her twelve children and sixteen grandchildren with a rod of iron. It was she who organized the family preparations for Christmas, and as we children became old enough to 'help', the weeks before 25 December became filled with excitement.

Pudding making was an activity which involved every available member of the family. Raisins, sultanas, prunes, cherries and lumps of sticky dates had to be washed and then laid out on large meat dishes to dry. They took days to reach the stage at which they could be handled.

Armed with a sharp knife and a basin of hot water, Grandmama sat in her wing chair before a roaring fire and expertly removed the pips from every single fruit. We children were allowed to grate the suet which came from the butcher in huge lumps. Horrid stuff, suet – so much skin on it – but not on our fingers by the time we had finished. The more responsible of us were given the task of beating the dozens of fresh farm eggs into a foaming yellow mass.

Eventually the day dawned for the mixing of all the ingredients. This was done in an earthenware crock normally used for the preserving of eggs. A whole bottle of brandy was added, and all the family came together at a set time to stir

The Market House at Godalming – before the Christmas rush.

the mixture and make a wish. If you could get the wooden spoon to stand up in the middle of the glorious smelling mess, then your wish was supposed to come true. I never did get the pony which I wished for every time for years. Fourteen greased pudding basins, fourteen cloths and a ball of string were used to make neat little parcels which were then placed in a scullery copper filled with hot water and kept boiling by means of a roaring fire underneath. The puddings were simmered for three days and nights, filling the house with a mouth-watering aroma and clouds of steam which floated about like a fog.

I use my Grandmama's recipe today, but my fruit and suet come from packets and I only use a small bottle of brandy. Somehow, my puddings do not taste like Grandmama's.

* * *

Although our family were quite poor, Christmas was always reserved as a very special occasion, small sums of money being regularly set aside throughout the year and paid into what was known then as a farthing club.

This regular saving enabled my parents to buy fruit, nuts, additional vegetables, joints of pork or beef, and generally a chicken as well – a rare and welcome treat during my childhood. Expensive gifts were beyond reach but inevitably, come Christmas morning, there would be a special something you had been hoping for in the shape of a coveted book or a doll or, in my brother's case, some additional pieces for his Meccano collection.

And of course our stockings would be bulging with inexpensive items such as fruit and sweets. A child's thrill on waking up on that special morning is not diluted or marred by the absence of wealth or sophistication, and my memories remain vivid and warm.

Evelyn's War

John Evelyn, the seventeenth-century diarist and courtier who was born and buried at his family home of Wotton, near Dorking, lived perilously during the Christmases of the Commonwealth years; 1649 to 1660. Christmas Day worship was suppressed, but Evelyn travelled far and wide to join like-minded people on the holy day – and on at least one occasion put his liberty at risk by doing so.

His entry for Christmas Day, 1652, is typical: 'No sermon anywhere, so observd it at home, the next day we went to Lewsham, where an honest divine preach'd . . . celebrating the Incarnation, for on the day before, no Churches were permitted to meete, to that horrid passe were they come.' It was the same the following year: 'No Churches or publique Assembly, I was faine to passe the devotions of that blessed day with my family at home.' And so too in 1654, when he noted penalties against observers.

The following two Christmases he went to London to receive communion from the brave Dr Wild; in 1655 at St Gregory's church and in 1656 at the cleric's lodgings. The '55 service was the last before stringent new laws from Cromwell banned Church of England ministers from preaching, administering sacriments or teaching school on pain of imprisonment or exile. 'This was the mournfullest day that in my life I had seene', the diarist wrote, but Wild was not easily

John Evelyn as a young man in 1641.

silenced, and the 1656 service at his home was so crammed with believers that by the time Evelyn had arrived he was not able to get near enough to the door to hear the sermon.

All of this must have been exciting enough, an adventure shared with a host of defiant kindred spirits. But the following Christmas of 1657 and its aftermath were a nadir of Evelyn's life. As a supposedly secret Christmas Day service was ending at Exeter Chapel, London, the building was surrounded by soldiers, with members of the congregation either detained or taken away after having had muskets held up against them. Evelyn was confined to a room, and when two colonels came to examine the prisoners he was given an unpleasant grilling. Had he prayed for Charles Stuart? He had prayed for all Christian kings. Then he had prayed for the

Winter in the woods in Evelyn country at Wotton, *c.* 1907.

King of Spain, who was an enemy of the state. Eventually they allowed him to go home, 'with much pitty of my Ignorance', but he had been shaken by the incident. Within a month his beloved little son Dick, just five, died of a fever aggravated by his desperate parents heaping blankets on him in a hot, stuffy room. Evelyn lived for the best part of fifty years after this incident, seeing fair times and foul. But rarely again did he encounter a period so traumatic as the Christmas of 1657.

Christmas in Old Dorking

CHARLES ROSE

This second recollection of Rose, a Dorking draper who was born in 1818 and died in 1879, was published in book form in 1878. Looking back to a time ranging from the reign of George IV to the earliest years of Victoria, it tells of a Christmas before Prince Albert had popularized trees in this country, or Dickens had helped make an industry of the holiday. The last line of the excerpt suggests that the link between smoking and painful, life-threatening illness was known to the man in the street at least 120 years ago, but as they say, there are none so blind. . . .

The Festival of Christmas, it is needless to remark, was generally observed in Dorking half a century ago, although as was the case with other old anniversaries, differently in some respects from the way it is now. Then, as at the present time, the approach of the festive season was indicated by fine exhibitions of beef and other meat in the butchers' shops, by shows of geese and capons at the poulterers, and by piles of pudding and dessert fruits, decorated with holly, in the grocers' windows.

The Dorking Town Band, which at that time favourably compared with the bands of the neighbouring places, heralded the season by playing for some nights previous to Christmas in front of the residences of the principal inhabitants. Then, too, were heard the waits, the most famous of whom were the Ditchling Singers, who came from their distant home in Sussex to sing the carols of Christmas. The leader of these celebrated songsters was the clerk at the Ditchling Parish Church, where even at the present day the musical part of the service is simply vocal, and where may be seen that now almost obsolete instrument, the old wooden pitch pipe – probably the very same that was used when the old clerk and his fellow choristers visited the towns of Sussex and Surrey fifty years ago.

Christmas carols in those bygone years were highly popular, and sheets of them, illustrated by wood cuts, quaint in design and rude in execution, were eagerly purchased. These productions were no doubt written by well-meaning persons, but some of them, it must be admitted, were anything but commendable.

Christmas Eve was a time of great merriment and activity – and, I am sorry to add, of no little intemperance. Then the elder wine cask was tapped, and this favourite beverage, made hot, was freely supplied to calling friends and neighbours, and to the customers generally of the trading establishments. The

Buying the family's fruit, turn of the century.

coaches which in the morning and on previous days had carried to London, Christmas boxes of game and poultry for cockney friends, now brought down distant-dwelling natives, and baskets of cod fish and barrels of oysters for country cousins or country customers. In fact at this time Christmas presents everywhere abounded, and the poor and needy were by no means forgotten. Then as now, at the mansions of some of the neighbouring gentry, the Christmas bullock was liberally distributed.

Christmas Day was ushered in by the ringing of the church bells and the strains of the band. The tunes of the latter were usually of a sacred character, but I remember the band playing on one or two Christmas mornings, forty or five-and-forty

A wonderful Christmas display at a Surrey butcher's shop.

years ago, the tune 'Get up! Get up! And Put the Pudding in the Pot', a reminder which some of the housewives of the period, drowsy from overwork, probably needed. Whatever some may have thought of this secular tune, it was certainly in unison with the festive aspect of the season, and not more inappropriate in other respects than the air 'The Girl I Left Behind Me', played by the juvenile fife and drum band on Christmas mornings of recent years.

On Christmas Day there was divine service both morning and afternoon at the Parish Church, the decorations of the building being of the simplest character. There was usually no service at the Independent place of worship, some of the attendants at which went to the Parish Church in the morning. At that period, too, it was customary for some of the congregation of the latter to attend the Sunday evening

Pillars of society: a town fire brigade in late Victorian times.

services of the former. The shops of the members of the Society of Friends, as on Good Friday, were kept open throughout the day, and their Meeting House, unless Christmas Day fell on their usual day of meeting, was uniformly closed.

The general fare of all classes on Christmas Day was the roast beef of Old England and the proverbial plum pudding; and around the Christmas dinner table was then, as at present, the happy place of family gatherings – although, as in some instances now, the vacant chair would call up cherished memories of departed loved ones.

The day after Christmas in bygone years was not, as at present, a general holiday. The trading establishments were all open, and their assistants, with few exceptions, at work. To the Christmas boxers it was otherwise, for the day to them was a high day and holiday. Then there were not only

specially kind inquiries after the health of the household by the postman, the milkman, the waterman, the butcher, the baker, the chimney sweep and by apprentices generally, but polite calls from, and wishes of, 'A Merry Christmas and a Happy New Year' by bricklayers, carpenters, plumbers and painters, blacksmiths, whitesmiths, wheelwrights, and I almost forget who else besides.

Christmas merry-making and a generous hospitality everywhere prevailed, and social parties were abundantly plentiful. The usual music at such parties then was not that now popular instrument the piano, but the violin, or as it was then generally called, the fiddle. At that time, indeed, it was thought to be quite consistent with the social status of the trading and even of the professional classes to engage for a party, or simply for the gratification of the household, the services of the humble fiddler and pipe and tabor player.

Two of the most popular of these unpretending musicians were fiddler Charley Cleere and piper Hilton, who played such airs as 'Auld Lang Syne', 'Home, Sweet Home', 'In a Cottage near a Wood', 'The Merry Swiss Boy' and other old-fashioned tunes. For the fiddler and his companion would be reserved some of the best elder wine and perhaps a piece of the Christmas pudding or a mince or Christmas pie to ensure 'a happy month in the New Year'. What became of piper Hilton I know not, but poor old Charley's fiddling career was, I well remember, brought to an end by a painful malady caused, it was said, by the 'weed' he loved so well.

Boxing Day Blizzard, 1927

MARK DAVISON AND IAN CURRIE

This excerpt from Mark Davison and Ian Currie's The Surrey Weather Book *takes us back some seventy years, to a time of massive drifts and a hundred tales of hardship and bravery. Imaginative thinking, too; by New Year's Eve the Salvation Army was organizing five aircraft to drop food on isolated communities.*

Christmas Day, 1927 dawned dull and gloomy, and for most of the day relentless heavy rain lashed down as families indoors tried to prevent the atrocious weather from dampening their festive spirits. In the murk outside, muddy puddles grew larger by the hour as the downpour continued, and roads were awash after days of unceasing rain. At Redhill there had been nearly two and a half inches (68 mm) since 20 December, and it seemed inevitable that serious flooding would take place.

What followed took most people by surprise, for as the light faded and a slight chill lowered the 46°F (8°C) recorded earlier in the day, the raindrops turned increasingly to sleet – and then large white flakes. By late evening, as relatives set out for their homeward journeys, carrying bags full of Christmas presents, a fully fledged snowstorm blew up. Even Surrey's well-off families driving brand new four-cylinder

Heavy going up on the tops.

Humbers costing £250 would have found the going tough as the century's worst blizzard began to bare its teeth on that wild Christmas night.

By midnight, savage winds whipped over the North Downs at Banstead, Reigate and Caterham, driving the snow into deep drifts. On Boxing Day morning, Surrey awoke to an incredible white winter wonderland – with scenes more realistic than those on traditional Christmas cards. Icy blasts of wind whistled through north-facing windows as horizontal snow brought white-out conditions across the county, piling the flakes into drifts up to 20 feet on roads over the Surrey hills. Boxing Day had a maximum temperature of just 32°F (0°C), and in the strong northerly wind, anyone not suitably dressed would have been in great danger from frostbite or exposure.

The following day, Tuesday 27 December, unveiled a

county gripped by the worst Arctic conditions known by its residents. Villages such as Chaldon, Tatsfield, Farleigh and Chelsham, near Croydon, were marooned for almost a week. Little children who ventured out at Tilburstow Hill, South Godstone, were photographed under 15-foot snow drifts which towered above them, snarling menacingly. At Reigate Hill, crowds of sightseers scaled cumbersome drifts to reach the windswept summit near the top of Gatton Bottom, where they were able to walk over the tops of sign posts and have their pictures taken by friends. At Effingham, a bus had to be dug out of a 14-foot drift, and in Kingston a man and a boy skied into the deserted market place while a snow plough cleared the road between the town and Winter's Bridge, Long Ditton.

By Saturday 31 December, fears were growing for villages cut off by the mountainous heaps of snow, and the Salvation

April snow at Batts Hill, Redhill, 1908.

Army chartered five aeroplanes to drop food supplies to isolated communities. The previous day a DH60 plane piloted by Captain Hope set off from Stag Lane aerodrome and circled over Surrey, but due to poor light it was unable to release its packets of groceries. On that day Croydon was listed as the coldest place in Britain, with 21 degrees of frost (-12°C) at dawn. The BBC asked people to lay out black clothes in the snow 'not less than 15 feet in diameter' to help the pilots pinpoint people in need across an area between Redhill, Lingfield, Addington and Sevenoaks.

The front page of the *Daily Express* on 31 December carried remarkable stories of the great blizzard. 'Glacier Near London – 8 Ft Waves Of Ice On A Main Road' was how the Croydon to Warlingham route was described: 'The main road from Croydon to Warlingham, by way of Sanderstead, which in the ordinary way is a busy omnibus route, is completely blocked by frozen snowdrifts for a considerable distance. It is impossible to traverse it even on foot.'

Vividly describing the scene, the newspaper continued: 'Mr A. H. Jannaway, owner of the Cherry Tree Fruit and Poultry Farm, Sanderstead, telephoned to the *Daily Express* office last night: "We have been cut off from the outer world since Monday night. The road from Sanderstead village to my poultry farm – a distance of about half a mile – presents the appearance of a glacier, the great waves of snow varying in height from four to eight feet. It is impossible to use the road, and Croydon can only be reached by making a detour on foot across ploughed fields and over hedges. The snow is even deeper where the main road continues from Hamsey Green to Warlingham. Efforts are being made at Warlingham to cut a track through in our direction, but the snow there is nine feet deep.

My farm, with the little cluster of nine cottages around it, is completely isolated as regards supplies of food by road. We made up a sledge party yesterday in order to get bread and

St Mary's Church, Reigate in snow, *c.* 1904.

meat, only to find that at Warlingham the bread was sold out. On our way we passed two other sledges, one bearing a milk churn and the other carrying an injured girl. It took us two hours to cover the mile journey. We also passed the tops of two carts which were completely snowed in. It was no easy task to get our sledge home, for not only was the surface of the snow uneven, but in places the crust of the snow was treacherous and we sank almost to our waists. We had hard work on the farm digging out the dogs in their kennels and clearing the snow from the chicken houses."'

Stories like this are remembered by a number of elderly residents in the district. Mrs Doris Cook of Bletchingley remembered, sixty years on, how as a young woman working as a maid at a large house in Merstham, she was terrified that her employers may not accept the snow as a reason for not

Winter sports on the Thames in Victorian times.

getting to work. Her father carried her two miles through perilous conditions so she could prove loyalty.

In Guildford, streets were buried under a foot of snow and the Hogs Back was completely blocked. Three buses and a lorry were buried within two miles of Guildford town centre. High up on Box Hill, hundreds enjoyed the sudden ski resort facilities. Some, it is said, dazzled the natives with splashes of orange, green, red and black in their costumes, built on the bathing pattern, with little caps and a dash of crimson round the tops of their socks. But the rain down at Merstham caused a landslide on the railway line, which stopped trains.

By New Year's Eve, many main roads such as the London to Brighton route were passable with care, although many hilly thoroughfares had become narrow passages between walls of snow up to 10 feet high, and the Bagshot to Basingstoke road was still blocked west of Hook in Hampshire.

Bean-feasts for the Boys

This church magazine report of the Christmas festivities of St Andrew's Church at Ham might well have been written in late Victorian times. In fact it dates from January, 1934 – and those Little Mothers and Little Cooks of the children's concert will still be on the right side of seventy; but what changes they have seen in their lives to date.

The Christmas treats all went off very well. The Infants had a very happy time. After tea, which was excellently served by the Misses Wells and their helpers, they had some games organized by Mrs Herbert. Then they pulled crackers and Father Christmas appeared and gave them all two lovely gifts from the Christmas Tree. The Upper School children, 150 of them, sat down to a splendid tea, and afterwards, through the kindness of our friend Mr Widgery, saw two excellent films.

About fifty of the Old People came along to their special Party and thoroughly enjoyed themselves. The Concert the children gave them was very much appreciated. I am very grateful to the Misses Wells and all the other willing helpers who made these parties such a success.

The Children's Concert: This has become quite an annual event now, and the parents look forward to it. Although January 1st, when it was held, was a terribly foggy day, the

Season's greetings from H.A. James of Esher, 1911.

Schoolroom was well filled with parents and children. The first half of the programme was given by the children. Miss North and Mrs Beagley had trained the girls, who gave four very enjoyable and amusing action songs entitled Little Mothers, Washing Day, Milkmaids and Little Cooks. Then followed a very pretty play entitled *The Princess and the Woodcutter*. Adelaide Buckmaster, as the woodcutter who won the hand of the charming Princess (Nora Haynes), played her part well. The King (D. Rowe) and the Queen (D. Worrsam) were all that a king and queen should be in a story book; the three Princes who were seeking the hand of the Princess in marriage, but were all turned down, were in reality Bob Rowe, Isabel Smith and Daphne Payne. Mrs Haynes and Mrs Buckmaster are to be congratulated on producing such an excellent show.

After the interval the Vicar presented the Medals and Certificates to the children who had attended the Children's Church regularly throughout the year; forty-six other children received certificates for regular attendance. A very amusing sketch was then given by the members of the Mothers' Union entitled *The Happy Portrait*. This brought a very enjoyable evening to a close.

The Carol Party: The Choir boys and the Vicar and Mr Barnes went round the village during Christmas week. We are grateful to those who so kindly supported us and are glad that our efforts will add about £7 to the Choir Fund. Many kindly asked us to sing in the house. The Choir boys enjoyed that best – because they had quite a number of little 'bean-feasts'.

Noel

JOCK VEVERS

This touching tale by the late Jock Vevers is from his 1991 collection Puttenham People, Tales from a Surrey Village.

I feel I must get down on paper the story of William and Mary Westwood and their son Noel, before it is forgotten. Perhaps writing it may stop the sadness that comes over me each time I pass what remains of Ash Farm. It couldn't be told much earlier because until all concerned had died it might have opened up old sores and made people talk. Not that it has anything scandalous in it, or anyone who behaved badly. Rather the opposite, but still, it might have caused sorrow to Noel. Now that he has gone, too, I think it is worth recording.

It's really a very simple story. I've always felt its poignancy because it occurred so close to where I live, and although I met only one of the three people involved, I have known the background, and indeed the farm where it happened, most of my life. The details, such as they are, came from neighbours and old friends, and though I doubt if I've got it all right, it's probably as near the truth as anything bearing in mind that Noel, even fifty years later, never had much to say.

Only once was I bold enough to ask how he felt about it after all these years. He just leaned on his stick, looked into the fire and then looked down at his boots and said resentfully: 'Dad shouldn't have done it. It were wrong, very wrong.'

Lying just east of the village, Ash Farm was at that time about sixty acres of not very good greensand. It has gone now as a farm, some of it for council houses and the rest taken by neighbouring farmers. . . .

William and Mary went in as tenants in about 1890 at ten shillings an acre, which was considered quite a high rent, for agriculture at the time was in the doldrums, with imports from Canada and the States and the new freezer ships starting to bring lamb from New Zealand. But the Westwoods worked hard, and I understand that William was a great hand with horses and that his ploughing was as near perfection as may be. They survived, and indeed prospered, at a difficult time.

William was a quiet, strong man who kept himself to himself, but whose advice, especially on horses, was much sought after locally. He is still remembered by a few for the quiet way he broke and gentled his horses. George Tremblett, the carter from Down Ashton, recalls: 'Billy Westwood was always kind and slow in his breaking. He had no fear; it's people that have fear that are hard on horses.' When he ploughed, William whistled the same three notes hour by hour; it was just his way.

He didn't like machinery. He never really took to the binder he bought when they came in. His pleasure was the single-furrow two-horse plough which needed just the one double-ended spanner, one end for the share boults and the big end to adjust the knife coulter. To the plough he tied this plough spud with its flat end and long wooden handle which he used to scrape the mould boards. I got that when the farm was finally sold up, and it hangs over my fireplace to this day. It's not much to remember William by – apart, that is, from what he did in 1918. . . .

Mary gave birth to Noel on Christmas Day, 1900. The date is important, and not just because she insisted on his being called Noel, a name that William found difficult. He would

rather have called the child William, like himself and his father before him. Name or no, William loved his boy very much, of that there can be no doubt.

In March 1918, this strong love made William walk into Guildford to volunteer for the Royal West Surrey Regiment. You see, Noel was coming up to be eighteen at Christmas, when he would get his call-up papers. William knew that if he joined up himself, Noel would be considered essential back home on the farm, and so exempted from conscription.

Both Mary and Noel protested, saying that it was a young man's job and he was too old. William, only just forty, said that was nonsense, and why should the young die clearing up the troubles made by the last generation? The rector had a go at him, too, saying that God had given his son to save the world, and that was the way it was.

William replied, and I know this upset the rector, that he never understood how God could have given his son knowing that he was to be killed if he really loved him: 'He can't have felt like I do about Noel.'

After a short time in Stoughton Barracks William went to France, leaving Mary and the boy to run the farm. He was killed while grooming the colonel's horse by a heavy howitzer fired miles away. They found him lying across the neck of the horse, both killed by the same shell.

When I take down the plough spud and run my hand along the old holly handle, gone like ivory now, with the WW burnt in, I can't help feeling what a pity it all was, and what a waste. Had William waited, he need never have gone, for the war was to end in November. Noel would never have been called up – for his eighteenth birthday, if you remember, was not until Christmas Day.

Fraudulent Folk

Two of Surrey's most famous characters of folklore have close ties with Christmas. It was in November and December 1726 that Mary Tofts of Godalming claimed to have given birth to several rabbits, apparently taking in a number of eminent medical men in the process. The case is often cited as an example of the credulity of those times.

A generation earlier, it was on Boxing Day, 1690 that William Davis, the highwayman known as the Golden Farmer, was hanged in chains on Bagshot Heath close to his home and the scene of scores of his hold-ups. The open lands

Mary Tofts: rabbiting on.

of Surrey were notorious for roaming thieves, and this mounted robber with a taste for gold was the most prolific of them all – even if, like Dick Turpin, he could not possibly have committed all the crimes put down to him.

Mary Tofts, the 'rabbet-breeder' of Godalming, was supported in her claims by John Howard, variously described as a surgeon or a 'man midwife'. The story was that the young woman had been working in a field near Godalming earlier in the year, when she had been startled by a rabbit. Soon afterwards she developed a passion for eating the creatures and sure enough, in November, according to Howard, she gave birth to her first litter of rabbits. There were more to follow in the weeks ahead.

The story became curiouser and curiouser. Sometimes the 'births' involved nothing more than the furtive production of pieces of rabbit flesh. Then, as so often happened with celebrated cases of fraud, events began to run away from the perpetrators. Howard happened to know an anatomist in the court of George I, a Swiss named Nathaniel St André. His true calling was as a dancing master and fencing coach, but he had read up on anatomy and had infiltrated the Hanoverian court mainly through the fact that he spoke German.

St André witnessed the birth of two rabbits and rushed out a pamphlet that quickly became the sensation of the day. But a rather better qualified surgeon in the royal court, Cyriacus Ahlers, took it upon himself to examine the case and found it distinctly dubious; so did the leading gynaecologist Sir Richard Manningham, who suggested that Mary should move to London to be investigated by more experts. She was installed not in a hospital but in a Turkish baths near what is now Leicester Square, and though society visitors mingled with the medical men, the truth was soon out. Evidence was given by people who had been asked to supply her with rabbits – to eat, she protested in vain - and the doctors who had

been taken in by the fraud became the laughing stock of the capital. Satirical prints and poems were on sale all over town, copies of many of which are tucked away in the British Museum.

On December 7, Mary confessed. It had been a hoax with the aim of making money. She was convicted as 'a vile cheat and imposter' and imprisoned, but by February 1728 she was back in Godalming giving birth to the more normal kind of human offspring. Years later, in 1740, she was sent to Guildford gaol for receiving stolen goods. And when a London newspaper recorded her death in 1764, all it could say of her was that she was 'formerly noted for an imposition of breeding rabbits'.

Poor old St André, the anatomical dancing master, bore the brunt of the scorn. He and the innocent folk of Mary's home town, who were 'Godalming rabbits' to the wags of Guildford for a generation or more. Like many a local jibe this was greatly unfair; after all, it had been the toffs from London who had been the ones really taken in by daft young Mary.

* * *

The demise of William Davis, Bagshot Heath's Golden Farmer, on Boxing Day, 1690, followed years of highway robbery along the great London to Exeter road that crossed this bleak, wild moorland. Davis reminds us of how people travelled around the country to work even 300 years ago. He had been born in Wrexham in 1627 but had done well in farming in Chipping Sodbury, just north of Bristol in the South Cotswolds, before moving on to Surrey. It was also in Chipping Sodbury that he met the well-off innkeeper's daughter who became his wife and the mother of his eighteen children.

What made him outstanding as a highwayman was the

Skulduggery on Bagshot Heath as the Golden Farmer strikes again.

double life he led – apparently unsuspected by even his wife and family for the best part of half a century. He was a model farmer on Bagshot Heath, a pillar of the church and supporter of good causes. It was gold that brought his two worlds together, because word had it that the mysterious highwayman stole only items made of the precious metal, and the respectable farmer paid all his debts and accounts in it.

He expanded into the corn chandlery business in London, and possibly 'went straight' for some years before bungling another robbery when he was seeking money to extend his farm. He was shot and wounded by a coach traveller who was as well armed as he was, and after he had been bound and taken to the King's Arms in Bagshot, his secret was out. For some reason, however, he appears to have been allowed to go free, and it was not until the autumn of 1690 that he came to grief, not on the wild uplands of Bagshot but the crowded streets of Southwark.

Now well into his sixties, he strode through the town waving his pistols in the air, and when some butchers and other men went forward to disarm him, he shot one of them dead and wounded several others. Bearing in mind the discretion with which he went about his business when he was in his prime, it is probably safe to assume that by this time he was out of his mind and unfit to be found guilty of murder. But as he had proved for decades, this was an age of rough justice, and after being condemned on December 18, he lived only to see December 25 as his last full day on earth. He was executed in Fleet Street, and such was his notoriety as the Golden Farmer that his body was carted off to Bagshot Heath to be hung in chains near to his home.

A famous inn keeps his nickname alive today, and there are those who say that he was once its landlord. That could well be true for the Golden Farmer, as we have seen, was a man of many parts.

Going Without Help

GEORGE STURT

This excerpt comes from perhaps the best known of Sturt's 'George Bourne' books about his old gardener Fred Grover, immortalized as Bettesworth. Memoirs of a Surrey Labourer *was published in 1907, shortly after Grover's death and at a time when the writer was at the peak of his powers. There is no doubt that he wished the book to be a memorial to the old man, and it turned out to be a worthy one.*

24 December, 1901: The next note brings us to Christmas Eve. The weather on the preceding day had changed from rimy frost to tempestuous rain, which at nightfall began to be mingled with snow. By his own account Bettesworth went to bed soon after seven, although even his wife urged that it was too early, and that he would never lie till morning. He had heard the tempest, and the touch of the snow against his bedroom window, and so had his wife. It excited her. 'Ben't ye goin' to look out at it?' she said. And he: 'That won't do me no good, to look at it. We got a good fire in here.'

Such was his own chuckling account of his attitude towards the storm when I stood by him the next morning high up in the garden, and watched him sweeping the path. He discussed the prospects for the day, rejoiced that the snow had not lain,

and looking keenly to the south, where a dun coloured, watery cloud was travelling eastwards, its edges melting into luminous mist and just hiding the sun, he thought we might expect storms. The old man's spirits were elated; and then it was, when the western end of the valley suddenly lit up as with a laugh of spring sunlight, and the radiance came sweeping on and broke all round us – then it was that Bettesworth stood up to give the sunshine his glad welcome.

A narrative followed which helps to explain his good spirits, or at least discovers the powers of endurance on which they rested. I said: 'We have passed the shortest day – that's a comfort.' He stopped sweeping again, to answer happily: 'Yes. And now in about four or five weeks we shall begin to see the difference. And that's when we gets the bad weather, lately.'

He stood up, the watery sunshine upon him, and leaning on his broom, he continued: 'I remember one winter, after I was married, we did have some weather. Eighteen inches and two foot o' snow there was – three foot, in some places. I'd bin out o' work – there was plenty o' work to do, but we was froze out. For five weeks I 'adn't eart tuppence. When Christmas Day come we had somethin' for dinner, but 'twa'n't much; and we had a smartish few bottles o' home-made wine.

'Christmas mornin' some o' the chaps I'd bin at work with come round. "What about that wine?" they says. So we had two or three cupfuls o' wine; and then they says "Ben't ye comin' 'long o' we?" "No," I says, "not 's mornin'."' Here he shut his mouth, in remembered resignation, as if still regarding these tempters. '"What's up then?" they says. "Come on!" "No," I says, "not today." "Why not?" "'Cause I en't got no money," I says. "Gawd's truth!" they says, "if that's it. . ." And I raked in six shillin's from amongst 'em. I give four to the old gal, and I kep' two myself, and then I was right for the day.'

He made as if to resume sweeping, but desisted, to explain, 'Ye see, they was my mates on the same job as me; and they

knowed I'd ha' done the same for e'er a one o' they, more 'n once.

'My old mother-in-law was alive then, over here.' He looked across the hollow to the old house. 'And they wanted we to go and 'ave the day with they. But my temper wouldn't have that. I says to the old gal, "None o' their 'elp. We'll bide away, or else p'r'aps by-'n-by they'll twit us." I'd sooner ha' gone without vittles than for they to help and then twit us with it afterwards, talkin' about what they'd done for us at Christmas.'

Mrs Beeton's Book

Epsom and Croydon have strong links with Mrs Isabella Beeton, whose publisher husband Sam helped make her a bestselling writer when he brought out her *Book of Household Management* in 1861. In its first year alone it sold 60,000 copies, while at the same time she was a busy writer of features for Sam's *Englishwoman's Domestic Magazine.*

Isabella certainly grew up with an insight into catering for large numbers, for she was one of a household of twenty-one children. When her mother married Henry Dorling, the clerk of Epsom Racecourse, at Gretna Green, each brought four children into the marriage – after which it only seemed right for them to produce thirteen more of their own. Though they had a house in London, much of Isabella's life revolved around their 'country' home, Stroud Green House in Croydon, as well as her stepfather's beloved Epsom Racecourse. When she

Isabella Beeton: a short but brilliant life.

married Sam at the age of twenty in 1856, the reception was inevitably in the grandstand.

It was a happy marriage, financially very successful – but tragic. Within twenty years both man and wife were dead, as were two of the four babies born to them. By the time the fourth came along, in 1865, they had moved to a home by the sea at Greenhithe, Kent, to ease Sam's tuberculosis. Little Mayson was the second of the healthy babies – but a week later the robust Isabella Beeton died of puerperal fever, probably caused by inadequate hospital hygiene. Sam was devastated by the loss of the human dynamo he jokily called 'master mine'. And twelve years on he was buried by her side at Norwood Cemetery.

That, in brief, is the human story of Isabella Beeton. But the only way to remember her is through her cooking – and at Christmas, what better recipes than this trio?

Nell's Christmas Cake

8 oz butter or margarine
8 oz soft brown sugar
1 level teaspoon black treacle
4 eggs
10 oz plain flour
¼ teaspoon coffee powder or essence
1 level teaspoon mixed spice
½ level teaspoon ground ginger
1 teaspoon vanilla essence
2 teaspoons rum or lemon juice
1 teaspoon almond essence
1 level teaspoon baking powder
8 oz currants
8 oz sultanas
1 oz chopped mixed peel
1 oz chopped glacé cherries
8 oz chopped Valencia raisins
1 oz blanched chopped almonds

Line a 7–8 inch cake tin with greaseproof paper. Cream fat and sugar well and add treacle. Beat eggs and add a small amount to the fat, beating well. Sift flour, salt, coffee powder and spices. Stir into creamed fat a tablespoonful of spiced flour, add more egg, beat well and add a second tablespoonful of spiced flour. Add rest of egg gradually, beating well between each addition. Add vanilla, rum or lemon juice, almond essence and coffee essence. Stir in rest of flour and baking powder, then dried fruits and almonds. Put in prepared cake tin and bake in middle of a warm oven (335°F, Gas 3) for 1 hour; reduce to very cool (290°F, Gas 1) for last 2 hours. When cool, remove paper and store in a tin for 2–3 weeks. Cover with almond paste and royal icing, using ¼ lb icing sugar. Cooking time: 3 hours.

Mrs Beeton's Large Rich Cake

1 lb plain flour
¼ teaspoon salt
4 oz margarine
½ teaspoon cinnamon
¼ teaspoon mixed spice
3 oz sugar
¾ oz yeast
3 eggs
1½–2 gills warm milk
4 oz sultanas
4 oz raisins
2 oz currants

Sift together warmed flour and salt; rub in margarine. Add other dry ingredients (not fruit) to flour and mix to a light dough with yeast creamed with a little of the sugar, eggs and milk. Beat well. Put to rise to double its size, then work in fruit. Put into greased tins (two 6 in or one 8 in or 10 in) and allow to prove till well up in the tin. Bake in fairly hot oven (380–400°F, Gas 5–6) for ¾–1¼ hours depending on size of loaf. When loaf is almost ready, brush over with sugar and water glaze. Return to oven for 5 minutes. Makes 1 large or 2 small loaves. Cooking time: 50–80 minutes.

Christmas Pudding Sauce

2 eggs
⅛ pint of rum or brandy
1½ oz caster sugar
⅛ pint water

Whisk ingredients in basin placed over pan of boiling water. Whisk vigorously all the time, until the sauce is thick and frothy. Serve at once.

Church Christmas Treats

We were perhaps never more fond of one another's company than in the years leading up to the First World War, when money in our pockets, increased leisure time and cheap public transport turned us into a nation of day trippers, music hall fans and Sunday evening strollers. Pubs, social and sports clubs played a large part in all this – and so did the churches and chapels, with groups and societies for members of the congregation right across the age spectrum. Here is how the hundreds of people associated with St Nicholas' Church at Cranleigh came together to celebrate Christmas, 1911.

Christmas Treats: The close of the old year and the beginning of the new one is always marked by a number of teas or treats in connection with the organizations for children in the parish.

The first of these was that for the children of the Parish Church and St Andrew's Sunday Schools, which was held in the National Schools on Thursday, 28 December. There were nearly 200 children present on this occasion and a beautiful tea, provided through the generosity of Lady Bonham, was put on the tables by Mr F. Winser. It is needless to say that the tea was very much enjoyed; but what always seems to be even more enjoyed is the fusillade of crackers which comes at the end of tea, the joy of finding little trinkets inside them and the donning of caps and masks.

During the progress of tea Lady Bonham visited all the tea rooms and said a few words to the children and received a hearty welcome from them. After tea an adjournment was made to the big room at the north of the school where Mr de Faye kindly filled up half-an-hour by giving selections on his gramophone. Then, when the body of teachers and friends had finished their tea, Father Christmas – truly a smart and jaunty Father Christmas on this occasion – appeared, and with a 'hey presto' caused the curtains to fly open and revealed the Christmas Tree in all its beauty. After a procession around it the presents were distributed, and then at about 7 p.m., after singing and cheering, laden with presents, oranges and sweets, the children were dismissed. Only a few of the elder boys and girls with their teachers remained behind for some games. The

Treats for all in Edwardian times.

Rector and the teachers would like to thank Lady Bonham and all those who contributed to the Treat for putting it in their power to give the children such a happy time.

Hazelwood Sunday School Treat: Thanks to the unsparing efforts of those interested in the Hazelwood Mission, a most successful Christmas Treat was given on 2 January to the children attending the Sunday School of the Mission. By four o'clock the room was crowded with a number of eager and expectant little faces. After buns had been served round, the prizes for Sunday School attendance and conduct were presented by Mr Brockman, in the absence of Mrs Brockman through indisposition; and after some carols had been sung by the children, the Christmas Tree was lighted and the articles with which it was burdened were distributed to the children. Every girl and boy received some gift, to say nothing of the oranges and buns circulated. It was a very happy and enjoyable evening for all concerned, and their gratitude is due as usual to Mr and Mrs Sandys and their daughter who give so much service to the Mission Room, and also to Mr and Mrs George Hook, Mrs and Miss Fortune and others who helped them.

The third of the Christmas Treats was that held for the children of the **Pittance Sunday School** at Smithwood on 4 January. Here, as is well known, three parishes meet, so that the Sunday School is not purely a Cranleigh one. The parishes concerned, however, all try to give a helping hand, and the treat is contrived between them. Miss Chadwyck-Healey made a substantial contribution in giving the tea, and the prizes and presents were supplied from various sources. This School is managed, as it has been for some years past, by Mrs Elwin of Willinghurst, and she is helped by other helpers; one member of the mothers' society going up every Sunday from Cranleigh. No praise can be too hearty for the work Mrs Elwin has done, and we present to her and to her husband and daughter, who lends a hand with the infants, our thanks for the

interest they continue to take in this work, and to all those who helped to give these children their Christmas Entertainment.

The fourth Entertainment – not one to be held every year – was that given to all the members of the **King's Messengers** in the Parish and held at St Andrew's Room on 2 January. This originated in the generous heart of Miss Ropoes of The Gables, who very soon gathered others to cooperate with her and by their combined efforts a very pleasant afternoon was spent. There were nearly seventy children present and tea was followed by games and competitions. During the course of the afternoon the Rector said a few words to the children, reminding them that their ideal as KMs was that of service, to give and not to get, and that if on that occasion they had received a reward through their membership, it was only in the hope of making them more diligent in their work of service.

Christmas 1952

Richmond was a good place to be a student in 1952 – at least if you were looking for a holiday job. We all remember young men and women delivering mail in their college scarfs – but just how many of them there were becomes clear when we read in the *Richmond Herald* of 27 December that year that some 400 casual workers were taken on by the town's post office, more than doubling the normal staffing level. Eight hundred or so people working at or from Richmond Post

Office! No wonder we have trouble keeping the nation employed these days.

What else was happening in the town that Christmas? There were wet carols around the Tree of Goodwill on the Saturday, presided over by the Reverend W. E. Thorp of Christ Church and the Reverend Elsie Chamberlain of Vineyard Congregational. The Rotary gave £25 to the mayor's Christmas fund as a result of this gathering, and there were more Christmas trees in the foyers of the Gaumont and the Odeon, on which patrons were asked to hang gifts. Rotarians distributed the Odeon's to poor children round the town, while the Gaumont's went to St Margaret's Children's Home in East Twickenham.

The films on at those two cinemas were two curious British offerings with lengthy and improbable casts: at the Odeon, *The Pickwick Papers*, with Joyce Grenfell and Donald Wolfit; at the Gaumont, *Made In Heaven*, with Petula Clark and A.E. Matthews. The *Herald* reported that a generous American was

A busy day in Kingston Market, *c.* 1950.

walking into one of them, went out again to buy a present for the tree, and missed the main feature. No doubt he has got over it by now.

There is almost a turn-of-the-century air about the paper's description of the busy scene in town in the days before Christmas. Can this really be little more than forty years ago? 'And did you notice the fine display of poultry in all the butchers' shops? Passing through the town after closing hours on Tuesday, it seemed as if every butcher was busy adding the finishing touches to the final displays for the following day.'

Indeed, such sentiments could belong to Dickens, and one wonders who was displaying the biggest, fattest goose in town. No doubt some of the prize specimens went to the major local hotels, where you could still dine handsomely for £1. And if you wanted to do it in style with a glossy dinner suit, Ralph Hughes from the aptly named East Sheen could see you right for 12 guineas; or £12 12*s* to you, sir.

Rare Recruits

A.A. BARKAS

Barkas was a great chronicler of Richmond life in the Surrey newspapers at the turn of the century, and his local history columns ran to thousands of words. Here he unearths parish records that tell of Richmond and Kew's embarrassing failure to

raise men to fight in the French Wars at around the time of Christmas, 1796. Perhaps two points strike us most forcibly in reading these minutes today. The first is the comparatively high bounty money the youths and men of Surrey were prepared to turn up their noses at – and the other was their freedom to do so, without fear of recrimination.

Richmond Vestry, Monday, December 5th, 1796.

This Parish, in conjunction with the Parish of Kew, having been required under an Act of Parliament lately passed for raising men for the Army and Navy to furnish nine able bodied men to serve His Majesty in the Army during the Present War, and the Minister and Overseer of Kew this day attending and agreeing to pay their proportion of the money to be expended in raising the said men, which appears to be a ninth part and a fourth part of a ninth. Resolved unanimously that Sergeant Simmonds be forthwith employed to raise the said men at the most moderate price for which they can be obtained, not exceeding the sum of Fifteen guineas per man, and that he be allowed the sum of Two guineas per man for his trouble and expenses in raising such men.

Monday, December 12th.

Resolved unanimously that a Bounty of Four guineas be offered and given to Volunteers to serve in the Supplementary Militia of this County for this Parish to prevent ballotting for the same.

Monday, December 26th.

This Parish and Kew not being able to get any men to serve for them in the Army at the Bounty of Fifteen guineas per

man. Resolved unanimously that a Bounty of Twenty-five guineas per man be forthwith offered and given to any able bodied man willing to serve for this and Kew Parish.

Thursday, January 5th, 1797.

Lieutenant Ruggles having attended this meeting and Proposing to find such men as this Parish and Kew may want to serve in the Army under two several Acts of Parliament lately passed for raising men for the Army and Navy, Resolved that this Vestry do agree to Lieutenant Ruggles' terms for raising such men, that is to say Thirty guineas per man and one guinea each for cloathing.

Resolved that this Vestry will meet on Monday next to take into consideration the necessity of making a Pound rate forthwith to defray the expense of raising the men for the Army.

Monday January 9th.

The Treasurer of the Poor Rate of this Parish not having sufficient in his hands of the said rate to defray the necessary charges and expenses of raising their quota of men for the Army, Resolved unanimously that a Pound rate of sixpence in the Pound be forthwith made and collected for the relief of the Poor of this Parish in order to discharge the said expense in pursuance and under by virtue of an Act of Parliament passed this present Session of Parliament requiring the different Counties of England to raise men for His Majesty's Army and Navy.

The Vestry of this Parish and the Overseer of Kew having made use of every exertion in their power to raise their quota of nine men for His Majesty's Army under the late Act of Parliament made for that purpose, and not having succeeded in raising more than four men, Resolved unanimously that

this Parish and Kew do submit to pay for the remaining five men the fine, or fines, by the said Act imposed under the direction of the magistrates in case of default in raising men for His Majesty's Army and Navy pursuant thereto.

The Christmas Present

CHARLES KOHLER

This story for older primary school children is by the late Dorking writer Charles Kohler, and was published in his collection Sunlight and Shadows *in 1974. At the time of publication he called his tales 'little cameos of life', and one critic saw in their simple, sincere quality a reflection of his Quaker faith. 'I'd like to feel that adults will enjoy my stories, too', said Mr Kohler. They do.*

Jack was awake. He listened to the slow breathing of his older brother, but it was too dark to see him so he again closed his eyes. He heard a whirring noise downstairs and waited for the cuckoo to jerk out of its box in the hall clock. He counted the hoots: seven, the same number as his age.

Now he remembered. It was Christmas day – and he might

get a clockwork engine for a present! He sat up in bed and groped for his stocking. He felt something round and soft: it wasn't an orange because it had no smell, so perhaps it was a ball. Then he fingered a long, cold, hard tube with a knob at the end. He pressed the knob upwards and was startled by a flash of light. When he pressed the knob down, the light went out.

He took the torch out of the stocking, pressed the knob, and pointed the light at the ceiling. A fly was sleeping on the lampshade. He swept the beam on to his football and then towards his brother's curly black hair.

Peter grunted and buried his head under the blanket. He felt warm and cosy and knew it was Christmas morning. He, too, was hoping that Mummy and Daddy would give him a clockwork train; he had seen a beauty in the Oxfam shop in the High Street. It had a chocolate-coloured engine with the initials 'GWR'. Peter poked his head out of the blankets: 'Let's go downstairs. We could peep into the kitchen cupboard and see the cake. And look at our presents. Of course, we won't open them. Then we'll get back to bed . . . You would like that, wouldn't you?'

'Won't Mummy be cross?' asked Jack. 'Of course not! Mummy and Daddy won't know anything about it! Come on – lend me your torch.'

The boys tiptoed down the stairs, finding their way by the bobbing light of the torch beam. They crept into the kitchen and opened the cupboard door. Inside, a big cake gleamed as if covered with fresh fallen snow. They looked at a plate heaped with mince pies.

'No one will mind if we each take just one,' said Peter, 'and a drink of blackcurrant juice, too. Mummy says it's good for us.' They carried the bottle and cups into the hall and sat down on the wall bench for a picnic.

'Now for the presents,' said Peter. Boxes and bags were piled on the dining room table. Some were wrapped in

Jack and Peter creep downstairs.

coloured paper, others done up in brown paper and criss-crossed with string. At the end of the table lay a large square box. Peter lifted it and shook it, and listened to the metallic rattling. It must be his train. He ripped off the string, tore away the paper, and took off the lid. Yes – it was the chocolate coloured engine with six carriages and lots of rails. He rushed into the hall with the engine in his hand. Jack followed him.

'Look at my train,' said Peter. His brother frowned. 'It's not yours, it's mine. Give it to me!' Peter's face reddened. 'Of course it's not yours, you silly. I saw it in the shop window and told Daddy I wanted it.'

Jack tried to grab the engine, but Peter clutched it in his strong hands. Jack kicked his brother and the sharp pain ran up Peter's shins. He turned and cuffed Jack. Jack yelled and they grappled and fell on the floor.

Mummy was dozing in bed. She woke when she heard the screaming, pulled a blanket round her shoulders and hurried downstairs. The hall looked like a battlefield. Both boys were crying, the crushed engine lay on its back and the cat was skulking under the hall seat, gnawing at a packet of sausages. The bottle had fallen over, and juice was pouring over the floor like blood.

She slumped down on the bottom stair. The house was quiet now, and the rising sun glinted through the frost-speckled window. The boys were standing side by side, looking at her, their faces dirty and tear-stained.

She waited, and anger slowly faded away. These were her boys, and her Christmas present. She laughed and stretched out her arms, and they ran towards her.

Nights of the Garter

From the institution's monthly magazine, this is the account of Christmas, 1926 at the Star and Garter Home for Disabled Sailors and Soldiers, based in a huge converted hotel on Richmond Hill. There seems to have been a stiff formality to some of the celebrations – the first Holy Communion of Christmas Day at 6.20 p.m. and a speech of thanks to the

governors from the inmates do not speak of a particularly relaxed regime. The Boxing Day concert party looks to have had its lighter moments, however, and its lengthy programme is reproduced in full as a reminder of the lengths to which people went to make their own entertainment in the pre-electronic age.

In the Star and Garter Home Christmas was celebrated with all the customary observances, in which both the patients and staff participated. On Christmas Eve a number of members of the choir of St Matthias' Church, Richmond, sang carols to the patients in the sick wards and in the common room.

Christmas Day began with the celebration of Holy Communion at 6.20 by the Honorary Chaplain the Reverend C.H. Maxwell, Vicar of Holy Trinity, Richmond. Shortly after 7.00 a party of nurses and orderlies went round the building singing Christmas carols on the various floors with most charming effect. Divine service, followed by a second celebration of Holy Communion, was held at 10.30 by the Honorary Chaplain in the chapel.

The Christmas dinner, a bountiful meal consisting of the time-honoured fare – turkeys, plum puddings, mince pies – was served in the dining hall, where most of the patients were assembled, and in some of the wards. After dinner Mr Harold Nelson, a governor of the home, visited the dining hall, and on behalf of the governors wished everyone present a happy Christmas. The health of the King having been drunk, Mr W. T. Ecob, one of the patients, thanked the governors and staff for their efforts to promote the happiness of the inmates, and referred sympathetically to the loss the home had sustained by the death of Colonel Grant Gordon.

During the afternoon the Star and Garter Jazz Band played selections in the sick wards. At 4.00 the dining hall was again thronged by patients and their friends, who partook of tea.

Boxford Mill features on the James family's Christmas card of 1907.

Both at dinner and tea a plentiful supply of crackers helped to enliven the proceedings. Immediately after tea the patients and their friends and many of the staff gathered in the common room, where they were entertained by Mr Phillimore and his dance orchestra, who played a succession of lively strains; by the popular conjurer, Mr C.H. Wells, who with the assistance of Miss Baldwin again astonished the audience by his clever sleight of hand; and by Miss Stafford-Northcote, a dainty and accomplished dancer. Among those present were Mr and Mrs Harold Nelson and friends, the Reverend C.H. Maxwell and Mrs Maxwell, and many others. At the close of the entertainment Colonel Gowlland, the Commandant, warmly thanked all the artistes for their great kindness in leaving their own firesides on Christmas Day to entertain the patients in the home.

After supper a whist drive organized by Miss Lawrence, the Matron, was held, in which a large number of the patients and staff and several visitors took part. The winners of the many handsome prizes were loudly applauded. The day's festivities concluded with an impromptu dance in the common room, which was greatly enjoyed by many of the staff.

On Boxing Day the Star and Garter Concert Party, conducted by Mr Davis, who holds periodical singing classes in the home, gave an admirable performance which delighted a great audience in the common room. The Honorable Sir Arthur Stanley, chairman of the governors, who had come down specially from London to attend the concert, in a witty speech, congratulated the Concert Party on the success of their efforts. Colonel Gowlland heartily thanked Mr Davis for his invaluable help. Mr Davis, in his reply, said he was very pleased that the Concert Party had acquitted themselves so well, and paid a tribute to the assistance he had received from Mr A. Shawcross, the honorary secretary.

The programme was as follows: Opening chorus, the Party; concerted item, Dooley's Farm, the Party; solo, The Sweep and Mignonette, Mr H. Medcraft; trio, 'Alice, Where Art Thou Going?' Miss W. Strange, Mr A.F. Davies, and Mr E. Redman; solo and chorus, 'Am I Wasting My Time?' and 'Two Sad Eyes', Mr E. Skinner; humorous song, 'Where Does Father Christmas Go To?', Mr C. Yielding; glees, 'John Peel' and 'Long Day Closes', the Star and Garter Harmony Six; selected item, Miss Collins; sketch, *Mrs Hamblett Records Her Vote*, Miss C. Mitchell, Miss Ford and Mr H. Medcraft; solo, Mr A.F. Davies; comedy duologue, *A Little More Soda*, Mr E. Moffatt and Mr C. Yielding; solo, 'Less Than The Dust' and 'Cameron Men', Mr V. Denham; duet, 'When You and I', Mr A.F. Davies and Miss Collins; glees, 'Men of Harlech' and 'Comrades in Arms', the Star and Garter Harmony Six; humorous song, 'Football Match', Mr E. Redman; concerted item, 'Moonlight and Roses', the Party; humorous song, 'How Does a Chicken?', Mr E. Moffatt; concerted item, 'Have One More Before You Go', the Party.

The enjoyment of the festive season has been greatly enhanced by the generosity of the many friends who have showered Christmas gifts on the patients. Special thanks are due to the House Committee for many extra comforts; to Georgina, Countess of Dudley, for her customary gift of holly and evergreens for the decoration of the wards; to Mr and Mrs Donald Dalrymple, who gave a present to every patient; to Mr Oscar C. Moore and other members of the tobacco trade, for tobacco, cigarettes and cigars; and to numberless other friends who have generously contributed gifts of various kinds.

Reason to Believe

MARGARET HUTCHINSON

The naturalist, writer and long-time kindergarten teacher Margaret Hutchinson was brought up 700 feet above sea level at Moses Hill Farm at Marley Heights, just over the Sussex border a couple of miles from Haslemere. It was in that town that she ran her Froebel school between 1931 and 1955. These three seasonal excerpts come from her biography Childhood in Edwardian Sussex, *published in 1981.*

It was said that when I, the eldest girl, was born, and my four brothers were shown their first sister, one of them remarked: 'But we wanted a proper sort of girl, one with hair!'

It was into the boys' bedroom one Christmas morning early that I had trotted, clutching my Christmas stocking. As we opened our stockings and cracked nuts and chewed sticky sweets in the half dark, one of the boys spilt the beans about Father Christmas. 'I know who it is', he said. 'It's Mother and Father, really.'

I did not want to believe him, but gradually the penny dropped, and being a matter-of-fact sort of child I was not unduly disturbed. The main concern was to hide one's discovery from one's parents, for it was well known that as soon as one knew the facts, Father Christmas ceased to call. Already George had stopped hanging up his stocking, and I felt quite sorry for him.

Dressed for the camera at the turn of the century: a family poses for the Redhill photographers E. Dann and Son of Brighton Road.

* * *

Toys in our family were somewhat classified according to their worth. Of everyday toys there were few, by modern standards. Building bricks of all shapes and sizes formed the basis of much indoor play, and of course I had my china doll kept well away from teasing brothers. For the most part we had the great outdoors and the barns. But come a cold, wet day or Sunday evening and we might get out our specials and play with them on the table.

Mother had many pieces of a doll's dinner service in delicate willow pattern china, and some dear little glass tumblers. These we got out very occasionally to be admired and then wrapped in tissue paper and put away again. I still have these pieces.

Who owned the Noah's Ark I do not remember. Possibly Father had bought it as a Sunday toy for us all. It came out after tea and we arranged the animals in the conventional two by two. They were quite large and well made in wood covered in what must have been real hide. How choice are wooden toys compared to the plastic of modern times.

An everyday outdoor toy belonging to Hugh and Mary was a low trolley big enough for one child to sit in and be pulled along by the other. This Father bought at Gamages on a pre-Christmas shopping excursion in which I was included. How exciting it was to see the huge store and to see Father actually spending a lot of money, for we lived under the impression that we were always poor and must not ask for anything. The trolley packed with other presents stood in the corridor as we returned home by train in the dark winter evening.

How good it is to return to the cosiness of our own hearth, particularly at Christmas time.

* * *

The grandchildren's party was no exception to the rule that the children had to perform for the benefit (?) of their elders and betters, and this was rather a dampner. For weeks beforehand Mother was teaching my reluctant self a poem to recite. One year it was 'When Polly Buys a Hat'. It was a stupid thing of three or four verses, and Mother insisted on my saying it with feeling, and with actions. My hands must go up to show the size of the brim; they must go down again and out at some exclamation. I forget the details.

But I knew when it came to the moment of truth that Mother would be helpless and I would have my way. My name was called. I emerged from the crowd of cousins and walked a few steps up the stairs and turned to face them all. Then with hands held firmly down each side I recited the whole thing in a perfectly wooden voice. Mother was furious, but it was too late. I had won.

All set for an outing in the family car.

A not too clever game we all enjoyed was Family Coach. Each one chose part of the coach set-up as his own: the front wheels, the whip, the lamps, the driver, father's top hat etc. Then one of the aunts would tell a hair-raising story of the family coach returning from a party. There would be deep mud, the front wheels came off (up jumped the front wheels and turned round), there was a pond the horse fell in, (up got the horse after a bit of prompting, and did his turn around), father's hat floated away ('hat, hat' would be shouted at some small child who had forgotten his part) and so the story proceeded from one disaster to another, including of course the highwaymen on Gibbet Hill.

Driving home on the dark winter's night after this lively end to the party was quite part of the excitement. We wrapped rugs round our legs, but the three-mile journey in our open dog-cart seemed very long, and more than one of us had a few shudders as we drove carefully past Inval Pond, where the road was narrow and there was no hedge or fence between it and the water. Our two oil lamps cast an eerie light along the tree-lined roads, and we thought again of those highwaymen of Hindhead who had killed a sailor and been hanged on Gibbet Hill, a spot we knew well on bright, sunny days.

Crow Pie Droppings

Crow Pie was described as the unofficial organ of the Ministry of Labour at Kew. In its early years, at least, it was both well written and light-hearted, and in December it did its best to turn itself into a portable Christmas party. In 1925 it let its hair down by publishing genuine letters of complaint the Ministry had received during the year. Pen-pushers in the civil service and local government are prone to such flights of fancy, and I recall my sister coming home with copies of similar correspondence when she worked in the local town hall back in the 1950s. Basically, it is a case of the educated in power sniggering at the disenfranchised poor, and not to be condoned. All I can say in defence of publishing this selection is that it was all a long time ago, the letters give us a glimpse of another age of illiteracy – and I agree with the Crow Pie *editors that they are pretty funny.*

Sir,

I have written to you four times with no reply and am disgusted. The mealy mouthed talker at your Bureau knows about as much as to what he is talking about as a fifth rate pierrot in charge of an aerodrome. If you don't attention my letters before the week's up I'll make things so hot through our local member of Parliament (he's dead nuts on red tape in the Whitehall dug-outs) you'll wish it were August again so that you'd be able to stand outside and cool yourselves.

There were not many laughs in bringing up children in poor families in the early years of this century.

Assuring myself of your best attention at all times, I remain,

Your most obedient and hard-up servant,

E— B—

Dear Sir,

I wish to draw your attencion as to my unemployment Benefit for which I have now signed for 14 weeks in the first place i have now signed on from the 7st of April up till the 9st of June and have not received no benefit nothing please Explain and state why so many people are getting it and I not I paid in the unemployed Cards from the first day they started so what has become of my Benefit please state at an Early date before I send up to the House of Lords. I have already put my

case into the prime ministers Hands now I require my Benefit to be sent on to me for the 22 weeks and received no benefit having spent all I am an Ex Soldier with a wife and a girl now I hope to receive my pay with apologies within seven days or further quarters I shall send to hoping this will meet with your approval without further delay there is no gap and plenty Benefit for all and if you have sent my Benefit to the Prime Minister he has still got it and without delay yours

Mr G G H—

Poperinghe Pashendale and the Western Front Urgent without fail or more will happen.

Mr Manager,

Concerning my pay which I have not got it is not sufficient owing to my wife selling a banana which I tell the man when he call that it is not my fault she is a big woman and got the best pitch in the Old Kent Road which when I marry her she give to her two sons what she have when her old man was alive and now she gone back again which dont do me no good without a word of a lie she saying I can draw the dole and she look after herself which is why my money been stopped five weeks and this is the truth so help me hoping this appeal will suit the comity I remain yours respectively

J— L—

Ser,

i sned a form at the Laber and the say come in a week and I come and git nothink and the say come on Weddensey and I come on Weddensey and the say come on Friday and I come on Friday and the say I cant get nothink I am diserloud ser why am I diserloud and if I cant get nothink why do I ave to

go to the Laber and sine a form ser it is not rite I should get nothink four times I bin to the Laber and the first time the say it is all rite sine a form and come in a week and wen I come I sine again and the same form four times I sine that form and I get nothink and then the say I am diserloud ser I am not diserloud I was in my last job five year the never say I am diserloud but at the Laber I go four times and the say I am diserloud ser he is about 18 and I am old enuf to be his farther ser it is a hinsult I am not diserloud ser will you please say wen I get my money bekos I go to the Laber four times and get nothink.

Yours respeckful,

M— F—

Out of work and out of a house. A family is evicted: what next?

Dear Sir,

I am writing to ask you I do not quite understand what you mean in this letter you quite understand I am a seafarer and I go away for 8 week at a time and when I came home you quite understand I saw these letters address to me which I do not understand so I am asking you will let me know what it is about sorry to put all this trouble down to you Ryde, Isle of Wight, but that is not my address as I was only stopping there for a holiday. I am enclosing your letter so you will understand trusting to hear from you soon I am going away again next Monday thanking you once again.

I am yours truly,

G— C—

Dear sir,

in defiance to my pay, dear sir, concerning my unemployment, dear sir, I have at present not drawn one penny from my local beuro for over nine months.

Dear sir, would you kindly look at my books, I here enclose my book, also the number of my book, also the number of my tally, dear sir, I think, sir, I write to the write person when I write to you, hoping you will take my case into your hardest heart, I remain in consideration of future favours,

Yours truly,

Mr J J S—

As above, being illegible to the unemployment benefit, and not receiving no mony for the period of 9 weeks before I went on strike, when I did not strike with the docks strikers, you can clearly see that I was singeing the card twice a day, and I am asking why I should not be entitled to claim a lowance

due to that respect knowingly, my fellow Brothers have drawn their back pay owing to the Dock Strike which you can fully see I was seeking unemployment at the time.

Boxing Day Hockey in Richmond

Richmond's Old Palace Club catered for sports as diverse as football and tennis, hockey and cricket, and its regular newsletter was a pleasing mix of fixture news and cheerful ribbing. This rhyme, titled 'Apropos of Saturday's Contest', appeared in the number of 29 December, 1903. I take the 'Little Mary' of the poet W.K.'s last line to be the female equivalent of the 'Inner Man', but accept the possibility that I might be perpetuating some more or less risqué Old Palace in-joke.

On Boxing Day a jolly sight
Could in the Park be seen;
A score or more of Ladies fair
Were sporting on the green.

All dressed in blue, around they flew
To chase the hockey ball;
The Palace Ladies dashed about
With many a slip and fall.

'Now ready, girls,' one damsel cries,
  The captain I suppose;
They bully off, she's got the ball
  And up the field it goes.

'Now keep up forwards! Centre there!'
  But 'Oh, I say, you backs,
Do keep your places,
  Else you can't defend their goal attacks.'

'Slog harder! You won't hurt the ball!
  Right up the wing, I say!
That's better now, then stick to it
  And keep the ball in play.'

They played their best, those Palace maids
  With all their might and skill,
But 'twas in vain, the game they lost,
  The goals they scored were nil.

The whistle blew, which quickly shewed
  That jolly game was ended,
And then along the river side
  To tea their way they wended.

Around the table they all sat
  With joke so light and airy;
The while with cake and tea they all
  Replenished 'Little Mary'.

Old Christmas Day

CHARLES ROSE

This last recollection from Charles Rose's Dorking book of 1878 takes us back to his childhood in the days of George IV, when many elderly people still clung to the 'old' Christmas Day of the time before this country adopted the Gregorian calendar in 1752. In that year, 3 September became 14 September – but many Christian traditionalists could see no reason why this essentially secular piece of legislation should have any sway over what they were convinced was the true birth date of the Lord. What interests me more in this story is its bridging of a time span of all but 250 years. My grandfather, who died when I was well into my teens, was a child when Rose was writing these recollections of people whose memories went back to 1752. Not many more living links of this kind would take us back to Shakespeare's day. . . .

New Year's Day was celebrated in Dorking half a century ago much as it is at present. Then, as now, the departure of the old year and the coming in of the new were observed by different people in different ways. The ringers rung the old year out and the new year in. Generally speaking, the ringing would commence but a short time before midnight, and continue only a brief period after. Sometimes, however, a thorough peal would be begun some hours before twelve, and would last till the new year had come.

These performances of the ringers were usually highly

creditable, for Dorking at that time possessed a set of ringers equal at least to those of the neighbouring towns. The juniors who succeeded them attained, under the leadership of Mr Charles Boxall, a still greater proficiency.

Some in the olden period danced the old year out and the new year in, others thought it more becoming to spend the last moments of the old and the earliest of the new year in meditation and prayer; while of course the majority of the population passed the boundary line of time in unconscious repose. On the New Year's morning and throughout the day there were the same pleasant friendly greetings and hearty good wishes as there are now. New Year's gifts too were not forgotten.

A village bootmaker's.

A street organ grinder with his small audience.

Fifty years ago Old Christmas or Twelfth Day was more regarded than in the present day. There still lived then some of the sons and daughters of the venerable sires who saw the alteration of the Old Style, now within a year of a century-and-a-quarter ago. These worthy representatives of the olden time used to say of this change in the calendar that they never would believe that their parents went to bed one night and rose the next morning twelve days older than when they had sought their repose. Hence, like the Russians do in the present day, they adhered to the Old Style, thought little or nothing of New Christmas and pertinaciously kept the old day – and as they averred, the true one. On the last named, therefore, they regaled themselves and their households with Christmas fare, and those who had cattle reserved for them on that day, the best corn and the best hay.

Twelfth Night was at that time, as it is now, the lottery night for twelfth cakes. For two or three weeks previous the growing number of iced and otherwise ornamented cakes in the window of the well-known establishment of Mr Uwins, in High Street, had been watched by the juveniles with intense interest. The appearance of the Head Cake was the sign that the eventful night was at hand, and with its arrival came a flutter of excitement which attained its highest pitch when the joyful cry of 'Prize!' or the depressing one of 'Blank!' was uttered. Generally speaking, on Old Christmas Day the last Christmas pudding was eaten, the last Christmas game was played, and after then the holly disappeared till the arrival of another Christmas season.

Chit-chat and Charity

This round-up of Christmas news comes from the Richmond Parish Magazine *of February, 1861 – a long, long time ago, with the Crimean War only five years past. At around this time the Richmond magazine was publishing appeals for shoes for poor children – and when the diary of events for the month noted a lecture on Dickens at Richmond Parochial Library, the speaker was talking not about literary history but a*

contemporary superstar who had yet to give the world Great Expectations, Our Mutual Friend *and* Edwin Drood. *Perhaps of most interest here is the staggering sum of £99 raised for the poor in an impromptu collection after Christmas morning worship – and the Dissolving Views shows, well over thirty years before recognizable cinema came to be.*

Seasonable benevolence: An appeal was made on Christmas Day, without previous notice, to the congregations of the Parish Church and St Matthias, on behalf of the poor at that most inclement season. The collections at the doors, and the gifts sent afterwards to the Vicar, amounted to £99 9*s*. A large distribution was immediately made in coals, food, clothing

A church group, turn of the century.

and money in the several districts of the Parish Church; and £15 was sent to the Reverend I.D. Hales, incumbent of St John's, as a gift to the suffering poor in that district.

The Old Sunday Scholars' Annual Tea Party: This interesting Meeting took place on Friday, January 4th. About 100 Old Scholars were present. After Tea, addresses were delivered by the Vicar, the Reverend I.D. Hales and the Reverend W.A. Large. Hymns were sung, and some beautiful Dissolving Views of Scripture Incidents were exhibited and explained; and also Scenes in the Indian Rebellion and late War.

Parochial Library: On Tuesday evening, January 8th, upwards of 450 Members and their Friends sat down to tea together in the Great Room of the National School, which had been beautifully decorated for the occasion under the direction of Mr Holmes. C.J. Selwyn Esq, MP, the President, in his address, congratulated the Society on its prosperity and usefulness. The Honorable Justice Haliburton was expected to be present, but was prevented by severe indisposition. A Musical Entertainment and Reading was then kindly given by Dr and Miss Selle, Mr and Mrs Etherington, C.W. Stockdale Esq and other gentlemen; and the whole concluded by the Vicar offering the thanks of all to Mr Selwyn for presiding, and to the thirty Ladies who had so kindly provided tea for the visitors.

Cottage Lecture Aggregate Tea Meeting: This took place on Thursday Evening, January 10th. It was a Meeting of all the persons who have attended the various Cottage Lectures held by the Clergy in different parts of the Parish. Nearly 250 were present, each District Lady kindly providing an excellent Tea for those under her charge. After Tea, Prayer was offered up, and a chapter in the Bible read by the Vicar; some beautiful Dissolving Views of Scripture Incidents and views in the Holy Land were then exhibited, and a short explanation of each given. Addresses were delivered by the Vicar, the

Reverend T. Sharp, the Reverend A. Garfit and the Reverend W. Bashall; and after the doxology and blessing, the people separated, all highly delighted.

It is pleasing to remark that there was a great increase at this Meeting over the numbers present last year, 250 being present, while last year the number was about 100. This shews a large increase in the number of persons attending the Cottage Bible Lectures, which is chiefly owing to the labours of the District Visitors in their several Districts.

In Drear Nighted December

JOHN KEATS

Keats composed this verse about happy nature and unhappy man on a doubtless drear December night at Burford Bridge, beside the Mole just north of Dorking, in 1817. He was staying in a little back room at the Fox and Hounds, now the much larger Burford Bridge Hotel. He climbed Box Hill during his fortnight's stay in late November and early December, but most of his efforts were devoted to finishing Endymion, *on which he progressed at Burford Bridge at a rate of eighty lines a day. From the tenor of this lesser piece, however, it is clear that he did not find solace unconfined in the wintry Surrey countryside.*

The brook, frozen but happy.

In drear nighted December
Too happy, happy Tree
Thy Branches n'er remember
Their green felicity.
The north cannot undo them
With a sleety whistle through them
Nor frozen thawings glew them
From budding at the prime.

In drear nighted December
Too happy, happy Brook
Thy bubblings ne'er remember
Apollo's Summer look
But with a sweet forgetting
They stay their crystal fretting
Never never petting
About the frozen time.

Ah! would 'twere so with many
A gentle girl and boy,
But were there ever any
Writh'd not of passed joy?
The feel of not to feel it
When there is none to heal it
Nor numbed sense to steel it
Was never said in rhyme.

Never the Same Again

GEORGE STURT

By the First World War George Sturt, better known as the country writer George Bourne, was entering the last dozen years of his life. Afflicted by strokes, he was by this time leading a life restricted by illness, and perhaps his bleak view of the world in general and Christmas in particular is not to be wondered at. He is certainly not the first person to believe he has seen a sea-change in the affairs of men, and swears that after him, life will never be the same again. So it has always been, through the generations.

25 December, 1914: No newspapers today, and we failed to get one last night. But last night a tale reached us from the town that newsboys were crying out news of a bombardment of Dover, or of bombs thrown on Dover. It is likely enough. The Germans seem to find a satisfaction in causing misery and pain not only to soldiers fighting them, but to women and children of the 'enemy' nation. And there is the reported doctrine of the disciples of Nietzsche and Treitschke to suggest that this malevolence is to some extent normal with the Germans; cultivated by them; part of their Kultur.

It must have been in view of this appearance that I began to wonder – on this Christmas morning of all mornings! –

Silenced church towers in the First World War. These are at Old Malden and Chobham.

whether peace with the Germans was even a state to be desired; whether we ought not to give up that dream, just as we have given up the dream of peace with wolves. The idea is too extravagant to be worth elaborating. I note it here simply as a sample of the sort of bewildered brain-work that too often occupies my mind nowadays, in the endeavour to comprehend what can have happened in Europe to bring up the present situation.

29 December: We spoke of the queer sense of discomfort the war is causing in our minds. As if people had omitted for a week or two to wash not their faces, but their minds. Everything seems mentally untidy, dirty, out at elbows, or like washing-day in a poky cottage. The papers contribute to this feeling, not only saying what isn't true, but knowing themselves to be saying it, yet hoping it will do for a time. 'Tis a makeshift, down-at-heels thinking. It somehow hopes that shams will pass muster for once.

30 December, 1916: Saturday Night. I wonder how many centuries since England allowed Christmas to come and go without the sound of church bells. Some of the dearest associations of old countryside life are connected with them. English country feeling – group feeling – is steeped in these venerable associations: but this year the parish bells were all silent, because of the precautions against air raids. And, owing to the war, there were few family gatherings; there was less railway journeying than in ordinary week days. The very carol singers seemed to be dispersed. During the whole season there were only three, or at most four, little troops of children who came to our door to sing carols.

I feel that Christmas – genuine old Christmas – has received its quietus this year. Imitations of it we may see in plenty after the war, but that tradition which the church bells helped to cherish for so many ages – jovial, kindly, pious yet pagan, only half-conscious of itself – that tradition will hardly

be recovered in the more intentional celebrations and festivities which may be expected in the future. They will be too intentional, too brainy. The genuine old Christmas was as spontaneous as the play of little country children.

Feeling rather than thinking these things while I lay wheezing and coughing in bed ten days ago, I was visited by memories of the preparation for Christmas which Will Hammond was wont to make in my shop, years ago. Old, crippled, stone-deaf, he had preserved the simplicity of the country places of his youth; and every year, as the afternoon of Christmas Eve began to grow dusky, he would put aside his work and begin, with the gravity of a child, quickly to sweep up his workshop and to set it in order. It was as though an unknown sacredness were at hand, and his place must be made neat for it; and so the tidying was done as a piece of ritual, a piece of piety.

December in Richmond Park

H.R. HALL

Hall was a naturalist whose book Round the Year in Richmond Park, *published in 1923, gave an enthusiastic account of the wildlife to be found there. That ring ouzel of 1909 must have been quite a sight. Today's bird books describe*

it as an inhabitant of hilly mountains and moorlands of 1,000 feet-plus, with no habitats nearer to Surrey than the moors of Devon and Cornwall, the Welsh mountains or the Pennines.

As in November, opportunities depend very much upon the weather. In times of moderate frost there is the chance of putting up a snipe in wet places. In a cold spell, common species, especially wood pigeons, blackbirds and thrushes, fugitives from the north, appear in increased numbers. Where haws are still hanging on the trees, grey missel-thrushes and fieldfares, of a bluer tint, are likely to be raiding.

It was a snowy day in December 1909 that the ring ouzel was seen on the plain near Isabella Wood. On another December day, when severe weather was reported in the

A makeshift sleigh in Victorian times.

north, eighteen teal were counted on the upper Pen Pond; and a winter season seldom passes without opportunities of seeing, on the same pond, the pochard and widgeon, which are perhaps the most handsome of British wild ducks.

Prison Food in the Workhouse

The Isleworth Citizen, *a penny monthly advertiser which counted Richmond and Twickenham in its suburban circulation area, was not at the cutting edge of radical thinking – but as can be seen, come January 1926, even a bland journal such as this had picked up on the fact that there could not be many more Christmas Days in the workhouse. By then, the Poor Law of 1834 was alarmingly out of touch with the spirit of the times – and three years on in 1929, in the lifetime of our Queen, it was erased from the statute book for ever.*

The food at the Workhouse, if we are to judge from the statements of some of the inmates, is not altogether of a palatable or appetizing character, and savours more of a prison diet than food for the aged. That is exactly one of the troubles about officialism that I have always set my face against. There are the so-called rules and regulations made by some body of

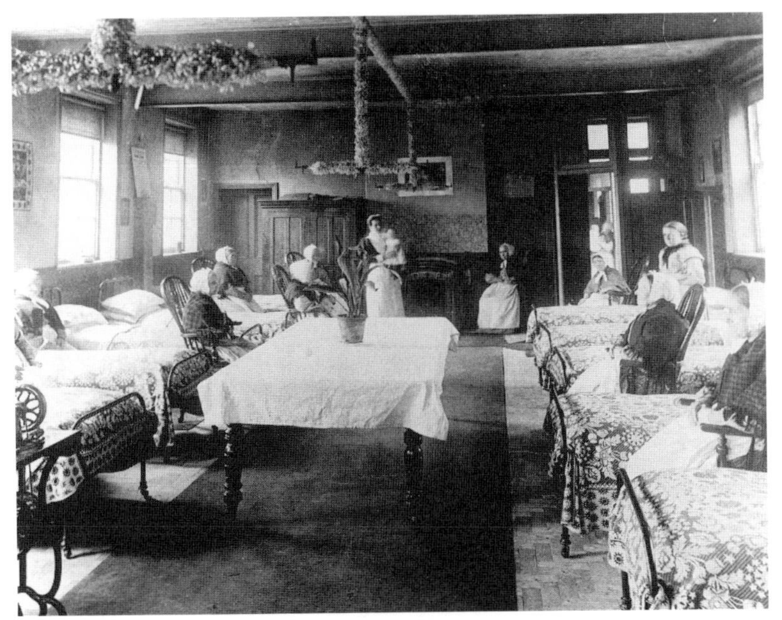

Old and infirm women in a typical workhouse scene; note the less than lavish Christmas decorations around the ceiling pipes.

men who know little about matters, and of course the officials must stick to the rules and regulations, or run the risk of being discharged. On the face of it, it seems absurd to have the same diet for old or aged and perhaps ailing people as for the younger and more able-bodied, who have a superior digestive apparatus.

But it is quite impossible to get common-sense rules to work in 'popularly controlled' public institutions. What suits one will not suit another; and if ever we are foolish enough to adopt Socialism or Communism, that is the way we shall be treated – all alike, whether you are big or little, fat or lean, healthy or ailing. Perhaps I may add that according to the

Guardians' official report, 'the committee are satisfied that the dietary as approved by the Guardians is issued by the master in accordance with the scales provided, and that no reflection rests on any members of the staff'.

The Great Blizzard, January 1881

MARK DAVISON AND IAN CURRIE

Perhaps some of us are veterans of the winters of early 1947 and 1963, not to mention the odd autumn hurricane along the way. But the real old-timers will try to convince us that we've seen nothing in the way of severe weather, and this account suggests that perhaps they are right. It comes from The Surrey Weather Book, *written by Mark Davison and Ian Currie, published in 1990 and reprinted in 1996.*

Described as the worst gale and snowstorm in any living person's memory, the phenomenal blizzard of 18 January, 1881, certainly ranks as one of the most severe in Victorian times. Shops were forced to close, vehicles were completely buried and a train came off the tracks.

Such was the ferocity of the snowstorm that the *Croydon*

Advertiser reported that it was 'the meteorological event of the nineteenth century'. The scene in Croydon was indicative of the type of conditions experienced all over Surrey and South London, with everyday life in a busy town grinding to a halt.

Caught in the teeth of the savage gale, Croydon battled to keep the snow out of buildings, but the millions of tiny ice crystals driven by such a fantastic wind forced their way into homes and shops and piled up inside.

An enthusiastic reporter on the *Croydon Advertiser* described how 'a perfect hurricane blew from the east-north-east and swept the snow about with boisterous fury'. The vivid account noted that 'it was not wet snow but small hard nuts of ice', and 'was driven with extraordinary violence against window panes, awakening those in slumber'.

At the height of the storm, 'the opening of a street door

Hostile weather, yet there is a strange beauty in these icicles.

A Victorian parson ventures out into the snow.

was a work of ease, but the attempt to shut it operated as a signal to the wind which threw its whole fury into the balance against the muscular powers of the door-closer, and when human power prevailed against it, the wind seemed to shriek out a wild cry of bitter anger and disappointed fury'.

Throughout the town, shops had to close as the blizzard raged on. At Croydon General Post Office the glass doors could not be kept closed and the snow burst in and 'careered around the clerks who stood top-coated at the counter endeavouring to persuade their cold and aching fingers to write'. The Post Office floor and counter were covered in a mantle of white and the snow even penetrated into the sorting and telegraphic offices at the rear, 'with remarkable and exasperating perseverance'.

At Smitham Bottom, near Purley, a van belonging to Mr R.F. Holloway, a Wallington bedding manufacturer, was

Winter chill at Alkham Road, Ewell in Edwardian times.

caught in the drifts. It was so deeply buried that three men dug for some time until any part of the vehicle could be seen. In Croydon, cabbies charged 'fancy prices' for travel. The railways came to a standstill and it took nearly three hours to get from Croydon to London. At Streatham, the last train from Victoria got snowed in and had to be dug out, and there were reports that the roof of the Norwood Junction Station had been blown off. Furthermore, a train carrying a few passengers came off the rails in the cutting between Kenley and Caterham Junction.

Back in Croydon, the northern door of the Town Hall could not be opened that night due to the threat of an invasion by snow. In Katherine Street at half-past seven, one or two members of the School Board met at the offices but had to wait half an hour for the chairman to arrive to make up a quorum. It was learned that Dr Roberts 'had been engaged in a hand-to-hand encounter with the elements for a considerable time while forcing his way from his place of residence in the south end of the High Street to the centre of the town'.

Croydon Theatre was closed on that wild and wintry night because snow had got into the dressing rooms. Mr Stanton, who ran the theatre, gave his company a night off. The next day, cabs linked to two horses overcame the deep snow, but double fares were charged.

Skating was reported on many lakes in and around Surrey, including those at South Norwood, Merlands Park, Wellesley House, Cavan Villa, Crystal Palace Waters, Princess Road, Mitcham and Carshalton.

The cause of the snowstorm was a deep low pressure system which joined a battle between warmer Atlantic air and bitterly cold Continental air. Winds reached gale force and gusted to more than 60 m.p.h., causing considerable wind chill to anybody venturing out of doors.

Petersham Scouts at War

The Scout Troop at Petersham flourished mightily in the First World War. By 1917 Baden-Powell's great youth movement was ten years old and as the war progressed, more and more little boys who had first worn the khaki as a Scout had grown old enough for battledress of a rather more earnest hue. These excerpts are from the December 1917 edition of the Petersham Troop Magazine, *and subsequent issues. The December number was full of the heroics of old boys, battle honours and deeds of derring-do against the Hun. It also made it clear that many of the lads would not be seeing their home soil again – but somehow, between the heroes alive and dead, one G.A.B. edged into its pages with a tale of 'failure' that it must have taken some courage to write. How glad he must have been when the next Christmas came around, and he was once again just another civilian among millions.*

I think about eight years ago was the last time I was on parade with the Petersham Troop; so many things have happened to us during that interval. This terrible war has deprived us all of dear relations and friends; though, on looking at the Roll of Honour in the Iron Room, I think Petersham has done its duty amazingly well. Many of the names on that board will, sadly enough, have to remain just names and memories to us when hostilities cease, for their

First World War recruits get fell in.

owners have made the supreme sacrifice in the defence of their country.

Far be it from me to quote newspaper cant of the wonderful deeds our gallant men have performed – yet I am intensely proud to remember I have known and shaken hands with those members of the Troop who have by their acts of sacrifice proved themselves heroes throughout.

Unfortunately, after eighteen months' service with the H.A.C., a Medical Board decided I was 'Na Pooh', and forthwith discharged me. The five months I spent in hospital prior to my discharge were very interesting indeed. The wonderful scheme for attention of wounded and sick men impressed me considerably. Taking into account the enormous number of men sent home from France, it is astounding there are enough fully trained nurses and doctors to attend the cases.

The hospital I was at had a surgical section where they were experimenting with the French system of healing wounds. The main idea was to keep the injured part

continually bathed in a certain gas, probably oxygen. This naturally involved a great deal of apparatus, but I believe the results amply justified the expenditure of time, trouble and money.

In my section the MOs were studying the eccentricities of that most important organ; the heart. The old accepted theory that any one having a gammy heart must lie down and rest all day has been exploded; except in exceedingly serious cases no patient is allowed to stay in bed after *reveille.* It would amaze some doctors to see men with Disorderly Action of the Heart and Valvular Disease doing drill and gardening or other light work. The men who returned from France and abroad after not being allowed to move off their beds at base hospitals and during their journey home were horrified at having to do drills!

This scheme of treatment has been decided upon by some of our cleverest specialists, physicians and Canadian doctors after three years' close observation of 'Heart Cases'; and in the majority of instances the results have been crowned as a brilliant success, results that the old treatment never produced.

My five months in hospital soon passed, however, and it was with almost a pang of regret that I donned my 'Civvy Suit', said goodbye to the hospital staff and returned to my original role in life. Personally, I don't like to know I am a 'Wash out', as the army would term me, but it is not given to us all to distinguish ourselves.

Nevertheless if we all do our individual best, and that best by modelling our efforts on the men who have passed before us, the result should be satisfactory. We have most excellent examples on the Roll of Honour board, and if we can earn the reverence those men have, we shall at the end not have lived our lives in vain.

G.A.B.

The next Christmas letter comes from one of the Scouters in France – looking back on the good old days in Petersham and, more chillingly, casting the little boys he left behind in the role of the next generation of England's manhood to be wasted.

Assistant Scoutmaster Bridge writes from France to say that letters from Jackson and Palmer have raised many longings to be back amongst us again, and says: 'I often think of the very happy Saturday afternoons and evenings which I spent in jolly old Petersham.' He continues: 'The weather is very severe, we have already reached 12 degrees of frost. The roads are quite impossible for horses. Nevertheless, of course, we have to maintain much horse traffic. My own horse skidded last Saturday, put itself in the ditch and me on the road; luckily we both got off fairly easily, the horse being apparently unhurt while I escaped with a torn muscle which is now well on the mend.

Couldn't get out of the trenches – a robust sense of humour in a First World War postcard.

'The importance of the Scout Movement has been even more impressed upon me while out here. The dressing stations daily show the huge wastage of England's manhood, and when one remembers that it is to the Scouts that we shall have to look for their successors, one realizes that no effort is too great and that we cannot afford the experiment of a slack Patrol Leader.'

Not all Petersham lads were heroes, not all were failures – in between were those members of the Poor Bloody Infantry who fought their battles, got patched up and then fought some more. Lance Corporal Wells, in the Alps via Monte Carlo and Nice, seems to be looked on with the misplaced envy reserved for the 'D-Day dodgers in sunny Italy' of the Second World War; serves him right that he's now so 'jolly cold'.

News of Old Boys: Private Walter Tibbals is now out of hospital, and we hope he is getting over the effects of his gassing.

Rifleman S.H. Coldman is still with his regiment, the London Rifle Brigade, at Blackdown Camp, Farnborough, where the weather is not ideal. But as he says, it is nothing to be compared to what the men have to put up with in France.

Lance Corporal Hector Wells has moved on with his regiment, the Queen's Royal West Surrey, to Italy. He seems to have travelled by the Corniche Road, passing Cannes, Monte Carlo, Nice, Genoa, which, owing to fine weather, was looking its best. He is now amongst the snow mountains, and we quite believe him when he describes it as 'jolly cold'.

An Inner Beauty

GEORGE STURT

From the Journals *of George Sturt, better known in his time as George Bourne, come these reflections on topics as diverse as the nature of beauty, the tastelessness of Christmas celebrations and our deep-seated longing for holly and carols and pretty girls. On the subject of the last, one hopes that somebody eventually came along to see in the apparently not very attractive school teacher, Miss Croome, something other than an abstract, impersonal sense of beauty. Sturt had watched her drilling children in the school yard and pondered upon a certain something in her favour.*

17 December, 1908: So once more an energy not peculiar to Miss Croome, had, as it were, effected a display of its own beauty, using her face and gestures and voice for its medium. As it happened, I witnessed another exhibition of the same sort of race-beauty, in quite different circumstances, latish at night. Susan had gone down to an orchestral affair at the Institute (Farnham) and I arrived there at 10.30, just in time for the last item on the programme. The leader of the fiddles (niceish looking girl, though inconspicuous in an ordinary way) was at the front of the platform; and in watching her bowing, so confident, so swift, so strong and sure and delicate and accomplished, as elbow rose and fell and wrist flashed, I got an impression of fine organic beauty which was really only a variant of what I had seen in the morning, in Miss Croome,

and the score or so of infants. In each case the beauty was impersonal, had no apparent relation to individual character; it was human life finding accomplished expression in the features and movements of individuals.

As I grow older, and discover better what I like, I think these impersonal displays of beauty come near to it. At any rate I do not find myself much interested (as I suppose Arnold Bennett is and as most people appear to be) in personal 'character'. It is not so much the differences of people that excite my appreciation, as the resemblances.

26 December: Look at the laborious Christmas card business, and the presents! See how thought turns to turkeys and geese, and roast beef and plum pudding. Consider the absurdities of mince pies, parties, and all the rest of it. The newspapers reflect the general idea-intoxication. Here is the *Saturday Westminster* with two ridiculous ghost stories, poorly told stories, yet 'seasonable'. Why should ghost stories be especially associated with Christmas?

The answer to that question would lead into groups of ideas – they have been sleeping for twelve months but are awake again now – connected with an older England where tales were the pastime of winter evenings, where the peasant and folk thoughts were those of everyday, and gave their quaint stamp to society. These ideas are of the village and the woodland and the country house, not of modern villa-dom. Our taste 'goes home', so to speak, into their atmosphere, and asks for holly, and Christmas carols – oh, and mistletoe and the thoughts of pretty girls and of children – so that the rejuvenation may be complete.

The Very Best Shop You Know

MRS C.W. EARLE

Mrs Earle's book of 1898, Pot-Pourri from a Surrey Garden, *is dedicated 'To My Sister The Countess Of Lytton, just to make sure that you did not run away with the idea that it was the Mrs Earle who served you your penn'orth of chips at the fish bar'. The 'Surrey Garden' line is deceptive. 'I am not going to write a gardening book, or a cookery book, or a book on furnishing or education', she begins. 'I merely wish to talk to you on paper about several subjects as they occur to me throughout one year.' And so it proves, although it must be said that the subject that comes through to us most strongly today is twee and outmoded etiquette. No matter, she was writing from another world to another age, and if a culinary man from Mars had to make a value judgment between our culture of pizzas and McDonalds and hers of fish kettles and ramekins, who is to say that we would come out on top? The first part of this excerpt reminds us of the sheer effort that used to go into preparing food. And as for the final paragraph, on seasonal hospitality, it is surely not far removed from our law of shopping nature that decrees that the most successful supermarkets are not necessarily the cheapest.*

An excellent winter salad for serving with wild duck and

many other birds is watercress, carefully picked and washed, pieces of orange, all the juice of the oranges and a few drops of good salad oil added just before serving.

Orange compote depends almost entirely on the goodness of the oranges and on the way they are cut. The best plan is to stick them on a fork, and with a sharp-pointed kitchen knife remove, at one cutting, all the peel and all the white. Then, with the sharp point of a knife, cut out all the pieces of orange between the white lines, leaving the white in the middle. Save all the juice, and cut small shreds of the peel without any white, put them into some water with sugar and the juice, and if the oranges are very sweet, add a little lemon juice.

Boil up this syrup, pour it over the pieces of orange and allow it to cool. This is a good foundation for any winter

A. J. COOPER,

Electric Machine Bakery,

40, Friar's Stile Road and 30, Hill Street,

RICHMOND.

Seasonable Specialities:

ICED 'XMAS CAKES, from 2s. 6d. to £1 1s. - -

RICH 'XMAS PLUM PUDDINGS, from 1s. 6d. to 7s. 6d.

FINEST QUALITY MINCE PIES - - - - - -

FANCY CHOCOLATES 'XMAS CRACKERS.

Silver Plate, China, Glass, Seating and Tabling, LENT ON HIRE.

Catering for 'Xmas and New Year Parties. Estimates Free.

Puddings and Cakes specially packed in tins for friends abroad.

The very best shop you know: Cooper's of Richmond, seen here advertising in 1914, aimed to be just that.

compote. Apricots, bananas or pineapple all can be added, separately or together, and a few dried cherries stewed improve the appearance. Another excellent winter compote is made by cutting up a ripe pineapple – often so cheap – stewing the peel in a syrup, to which is added the juice that runs out of the pineapple and a little ginger. Strain, and pour it boiling over the pieces of pineapple. A few bananas cut up and added to the pineapple, improve it.

Two excellent ways of serving cold chicken for small parties or suppers are the following. Order the day before from a good baker some extra small dinner rolls, cut off the tops and take out the crumb. Mince a little chicken and ham or tongue; it takes a very small quantity of either. Mix with well-made Mayonnaise sauce, a little chopped parsley and a very little onion. Put this into the rolls and replace the small round top on each. Finger rolls, cut in half and the crumb taken out, can be done in the same way.

The other way is to make some little open sandwiches – we call them Barrington sandwiches – in the following manner. Butter some moderately thick slices of a good tin loaf and cut them into medium-sized rounds. Lay across them, in pieces cut quite narrow, some breast of cold chicken, a quarter of an anchovy and a thin shred of green gherkin. These form narrow bars of green, white, and red across the slices of bread. Trim the edges, and serve on a plate one laid partly over the other, like cutlets.

I particularly want to say a last word to housekeepers who are anxious to indulge in hospitality. Hospitality should mean, to my mind, not altering our whole way of living, but giving the best of our habitual food. For this, nothing is so telling, whether the dinner be large or small, as the procuring of some special seasonable luxury. It is well worth taking the trouble to get any such luxuries not from the usual shop in your neighbourhood, but from the very best shop you know of

for each speciality, whether fish, game, vegetable, Italian goods more especially, fruit (fresh or bottled), dessert, biscuits or cake. The really good housekeeper is alert to learn where the best things come from, and to take hints wherever she goes. One should never through idleness give up getting the best things. If you go to the expense of entertaining at all, it makes little difference in the way of money whether you deal at a specially good shop or a second-rate one, and the results at your table are very different indeed.

Wraiths at the Rectory

FRANCES D. STEWART

More spooky goings-on from the pen of Frances Stewart, this time taken from her book Around Haunted Croydon, *first published in 1989.*

Now completely renovated and used as offices by a commercial firm, the Old Rectory at Caterham-on-the-Hill must surely be the most haunted house in the district. Dating in part from the sixteenth century, it was once in the possession of Waltham Abbey. Though hauntings may have begun earlier, the record of mysterious circumstances starts at

the beginning of this century with the Reverend Alick St John Heard and his wife, who moved into the rectory when his father Prebendary Heard retired to the West Country.

To begin with, they could hear footsteps going along the first floor corridor when they were alone in the house. Puzzling as this was, more curious events were to follow. They so often found doors open when they knew for sure that they had been closed that the Rector decided to conduct an experiment. He locked every door securely, then he and his wife went out, taking the keys with them. On their return about an hour later, they found every door wide open.

One day Mrs Heard was in the bathroom, at the end of the first floor corridor, and she heard approaching footsteps and the rattle of the door knob. Believing someone to be there she called out, but there was no reply. She went to open the door but was prevented from doing so as it seemed as if it was being held on the outside. She persevered, and after an almighty tug the door flew inwards, revealing an empty corridor. Another time, as she was about to leave the bathroom the door suddenly slammed shut in her face for no apparent reason. Next to the bathroom was a bedroom with two huge bolts and a metal bar which slotted across on the inside. Obviously a previous occupant had wanted to keep someone or something out. When this bedroom was being decorated some years later, the painter, who came from another area and knew nothing about the ghost, found the atmosphere so depressing that he could not work in it for any length of time without having a break to restore his nerves.

The Rector employed a resident housekeeper with two children, all of whom were repeatedly made aware of the supernatural presence. One evening the Heards were going out and they asked the housekeeper to put their supper on the table as soon as they returned. When they arrived home, they were surprised and somewhat annoyed to find the meal

Atmospheric: the Old Rectory at Caterham.

already on the table and getting cold. They called the housekeeper to complain, but she apologised and said that she was sure she had heard them walking about upstairs some time before.

On another occasion, a lady arrived at the front door saying that she had come to receive religious instruction from the Rector. The housekeeper said that as he was out, she was welcome to come in and wait until he returned. No sooner had she sat down than an elderly gentleman entered, had some brief conversation with her and left. When the Rector returned she described the visitor to him, but he was completely perplexed and said he had no knowledge of such a person. When asked, the housekeeper said she had admitted nobody but the young lady.

Another extraordinary incident took place when Mr Heard was called away to visit his father, who was desperately ill. During his absence, the verger was talking to an acquaintance in the churchyard when he was surprised to see the figure of the Rector's father enter the mortuary. Having a lot on his mind at the time, the verger forgot the incident, but a day or so later he was told that the sick man had died at his home at exactly the same time as he was seen to enter the mortuary. Shortly after, the son of the housekeeper, sleeping in his own room at the rectory, awoke to find the ghost of Prebendary Heard rummaging through some papers at the end of the bed. Why had his ghost returned to the Rectory? Had he left something important behind him when he retired so long ago?

Over the years, both the Heards and their housekeeper became accustomed to their ghosts. Although no positive description was given of any of them, a gentleman who spent a few nights there expressed his regret to a friend that he had slept so well that he had missed seeing the ghost believed to be a hooded figure resembling a monk.

When Mr Heard retired he was succeeded by a Dr Butterworth, who maintained that at no time did he experience anything unusual. With the arrival of the next Rector, the Reverend Kenneth Budd, the mysterious activities resumed. Although he and his wife were sceptical at first, it was not long before they had reason to change their minds.

The Rectory had been converted to flats, with the Rector living on the first floor and an engineer and his family living below. One day Mr Budd returned to the house with a friend, only to find Mrs Budd had gone out, taking the key with her; they had no alternative but to wait for her return. Whilst standing on the lawn, they saw what appeared to be people moving around upstairs. They hurried over to check the doors in case they had not noticed Mrs Budd return, but they were

still locked. When Mrs Budd did arrive they conducted a thorough search, but found no one on the premises.

The engineer told the architect responsible for the alterations to the building that he often heard footsteps going along the first floor corridor when the Rector was out, and that his family, too, repeatedly found doors that they had locked wide open on their return. He said that one day when his wife was working on the hearth in front of the fireplace, she heard someone enter the room. Presuming it to be her husband she turned round to see what he wanted, but found she was quite alone and the door still closed.

So much supernatural activity took place that the engineer's daughter decided to call in a medium. After spending some time in the house, she said that she felt it had been used as a resting place for monks on long journeys. Something had gone wrong during one of their visits and a bell had been buried on the premises, for which a monk had been searching ever since.

The Rector and his wife moved to a newly-built Rectory, and the engineer's family left. A new occupant was found for the upper flat, but the ground floor remained empty for a long time before it received new tenants. These were a family of four children and their mother. The first horrors they had to contend with were those of damp and dry rot, so builders were soon called in.

Whilst the necessary repairs were being executed, the mother slept in the hall. One night she awoke with a start to find herself in a cold sweat. She was sure somebody was standing over her. Though too terrified to turn on the light, she was convinced it was a tall, hooded figure. The next day she told the builder, who said he was not at all surprised. He said the house had a depressing atmosphere, especially at the back. Not wanting to scare the children, she did not mention it to them, but it wasn't long before they had stories to tell

her. The son, who slept at the end of the hall, said that he had heard footsteps approaching and had seen the bedroom handle move, but nobody entered. He refused to sleep in the room again unless accompanied by his dog. The youngest daughter saw what she thought was a monk pass the side window. Thinking it was a visitor she went to let him in, but he had vanished. They often thought they heard the back door open, but their welcoming calls would bring no response.

Eventually the mother remarried, and the husband joined the family in the Rectory. This in no way deterred the resident spirits. The husband's first encounter was when he was sitting alone one evening watching television. On the sideboard was a deep glass fruit bowl, at the bottom of which were a few apples. His viewing was distracted by a dull thud, and on looking towards the sideboard he saw one of the apples rolling across the floor, apparently having lifted itself out of the bowl. He did not stop to look for an explanation but rushed from the room, and was glad when the family returned.

Though they continued to be disturbed by some of the happenings, particularly those that occurred at the back of the house where it was constantly cold, they began to be amused by the more bizarre events. One evening as one of the teenage girls sat alone in the house with her boyfriend, they saw a pair of shoes walk, as if worn by some unseen person, from one side of the room to the other. Another time the mother expected to hear howls of disgust when her son came in from work to discover that the shoes he had ordered from a mail order company were a quite hideous colour. When nothing happened she tip-toed to his room, but he wasn't there. So who had walked up the hall and into his bedroom? Frequently small articles such as hair brushes would seem to move of their own accord, and the dog would have bouts of restlessness, wandering from room to room as if following

someone. The family named the friendly ghost Alfie, but preferred to keep anonymous the sinister 'something' that lurked in the shadows at the back of the house.

The occupants of the first floor flat were no less troubled than the family below. They too found objects would move without explanation. On returning from a holiday they found all the windows of their flat open. Pleased at first, as they had asked a friend to air the rooms, they were less pleased when he hurried up the drive behind them apologising profusely for being so late in attending to the task. Inside, nothing had been taken or disturbed, although the family below had heard footsteps, furniture being moved about, and on one occasion what sounded like a pile of books crashing to the floor.

Another medium visited the house, and like the previous one, said it had been used as a hostelry. She declared the front of the building to be possessed by the spirits of good and those at the back to be evil. She said that she felt some body

No ghosts in sight, but an oddly chilling winter's scene at Waller Lane, Caterham.

or bodies to be buried in close proximity to the house, and I have information from another source which says a skeleton was recovered from a shallow grave by the back door. Perhaps it was a child's grave, as a medium said she could see a figure of a child in Victorian costume following one of the daughters around the house.

Close neighbours have their own stories about the building, and one concerns a young lady who lived there many years ago. She is said to have been a brilliant pianist who became desperately ill. When she died, her lover was so distraught that he committed suicide. Since then, haunting music has been heard drifting across the gardens when the house was unoccupied.

I recently revisited the Old Rectory. To see it now makes it difficult to believe it was haunted, but I knew it before the decorators got to work. I remember an old oak door studded with nails, one for every person who died when the Plague hit Caterham. I have seen the mists swirl round the ancient apple tree, and felt the damp chill rise from the cellar. But mostly I remember the warm atmosphere at Christmas time, when a huge, traditionally decorated tree stood twinkling by the hearth, and the New Year parties that had all the right ingredients, good food, good company and the perfect hosts.

Those days have gone and the spirits with them; or have they? For who knows what happens after the staff have left at night, and before they return in the morning?

My last story comes from the Warlingham area. It is a tale for telling at Christmas time, preferably when the listeners are seated together round a glowing fire. A lady who moved into her house in Farleigh Road about twenty years ago told me that she soon noticed that local residents always referred to one section of the road as Baker's Hill. When she asked an elderly neighbour the reason for this, she was very surprised at the following explanation.

Apparently there was a bakery in the vicinity, from which the baker's boy regularly walked to Selsdon to deliver to customers. One day as he passed some trees on the bend of the road he was set upon by a woodman wielding an axe, who hacked him to death. Apart from a nervous glance towards the trees on Baker's Hill whenever she was passing, the lady gave no more thought to the story. But some years later her daughter, who was resident in Selsdon, said that some neighbours had experienced a very frightening encounter. It happened on Boxing Day, when the neighbour drove his father and son to Westerham. A thick grey fog clung to the trees and brushed against the car as they motored up Farleigh Road. Suddenly, a dark shape loomed up in front of them and the headlights revealed the figure of a tall man wearing a country style suit and carrying an axe in his right hand. The driver slammed on his brakes and jumped out of the car to shout at the man for being in the road and endangering all their lives, but he had vanished. Nothing was to be seen but the trees dripping with moisture as they hung over the open road. All three passengers had seen the apparition and were so shaken that they used an alternative route on the return journey in order to avoid a second encounter.

When the lady told another elderly resident about the family's ordeal, she said that her mother had been seventeen years old at the time of the murder and had told her the exact tree where the axe had been hidden. Since then, whenever she had passed that spot with her dog, he had panicked and run as if his life was threatened. Fortunately for today's motorists, the trees have now been removed and the road widened, making driving easier and ghosts less likely.

Swinging Sixties

Members of the baby boom generation - those born around the end of the Second World War – have a special affection for the middle and late 1960s, when they were in their early twenties. It was a magical time, they always say – yet if you look at the newspapers from then, especially the local weeklies, it is usually hard to pick up on the vibrations of those years. Their columns are filled, as they were ten, twenty and fifty years before, with Women's Institute meetings, motoring offences and the council's deliberations over roads, footpaths and sewers. Only in the entertainments guide, where groovy beat groups replace the syncopating combos of earlier times, do you pick up on the new world throbbing out there. But surely the Age of Aquarius was about more than pop music? At the time, the baby boomers certainly thought so – but today, who knows?

Looking at the *Surrey Advertiser* of Friday, 20 December 1968, only one news story reflects the era of love and peace – a two-day inquiry into the running of the Guildford School of Art by a House of Commons sub-committee on education and science after a sit-in at the college earlier that year. It was in 1968 that students tore up the cobblestones of Paris to hurl at police in a summer of protest. The spirit of the times, after the happy optimism of the middle of the decade, was turning to one of muddled anarchic revolution, all played out against a background of an increasing use of LSD and cannabis and the rising death toll of the Vietnam War – the baby boomers of America bore the brunt of this conflict. The average age of GIs killed in the war was just nineteen.

All of this was a long way away from Guildford, but in retrospect, the protests of 1968 were not so futile as they first seemed. Although the Vietnam War did not end until 1975, it was in '68 that President Johnson, alarmed both by the deaths of Americans and by increasingly bitter protests against them, ordered Henry Kissinger to begin negotiations with the North Vietnamese. Johnson was concerned about his standing in Middle America, but the leafy middle-class suburbs would not have latched on to the issue nearly so quickly without the outcry of the baby boomers' peace movement.

Things were not like, er, so heavy, man, at Guildford School of Art, but there was clearly concern about what was seen by many at the time as an over-liberal regime. One of the main headlines of the *Surrey Advertiser* report read: 'Students And Junior Staff On Christian Name Terms. 'On such shifting sands were revolutions founded some thirty years ago. How quaint it seems, yet I know from personal experience that at the time, issues like that really did matter. I recall when I was a grammar school sixth-former, not five years before the Guildford sit-in, one of our more relaxed young teachers took to addressing some of us older boys, perhaps six or seven years his junior, by our first names; we derided him and shrunk away from him as if he had made an indecent suggestion.

There was another sign of times a-changing with the report that the Chiddingfold Farmers would cease to hunt a pack of foxhounds from the end of the season. They had been around since 1943, and traffic, urbanization and electric railways were cited as the main reasons for their demise. Another piece of Chiddingfold news was the departure of the Wellses as landlords of the Swan after fourteen years.

It was an unhappy Christmas for a Haslemere motorist aged eighty-four, who collided with a motorbike at Shottermill and was fined £15 and had his licence endorsed. Magistrates were doubtless mindful that this was not the first

blot on his copybook; he had been up before them sixty-three years earlier, in 1905.

In a Christmas experiment, Guildford's four Congregational churches were getting together for a new Nativity play and a festival of modern carols. There were special events at two of the churches – Portsmouth Road, Westborough and St Peter's, Bellfield.

Some 1968 prices: in Plummers of Guildford's food hall, oven-ready turkeys weighing up to 15 lb were to be had at 3*s* 11*d* per pound, while English leg of pork was 4*s* 6*d* a pound. Three-piece suites at Thomas Wallis's in Guildford High Street were 69 guineas, and you could buy an almost new Rolls-Royce Silver Shadow in regal red, one owner, for £7,850. A two-year-old Triumph 2000 in cactus, again one owner, was yours for £875.

There were some familiar names at the local cinemas: Woking Odeon was still showing *The Sound of Music*, which by 1968 was beginning to give the impression that it would never close. *The Belles of St Trinians* and *Dr Who and the Daleks* were an unlikely but appealing combination at Guildford Astor, and then, as now, there were festive Disneys everywhere. The Rex at Haslemere was showing *The Jungle Book* and *Wind in the Willows*, and at the Regal in Cranleigh, *Lady and the Tramp* was teamed with *Sammy the Way-out Seal.*

Starring at Guildford Civic Hall, the American P.P. Arnold was belting out her two Top Thirty hits of the previous eighteen months, 'First Cut is the Deepest' and 'Angel of the Morning'. She has not been back in the British charts since Christmas 1968, but such is her stage presence that she is still filling venues far larger than Guildford Civic Hall.

At the Mad Gin Mill at the Angel, Godalming, the big Christmas draw was the group Black Cat Bones. Yes, exactly – but it was a case of jam tomorrow, since the likes of Fleetwood Mac and Alexis Korner were lined up to appear there in 1969.

There was more twisting to be done at the Stoke Hotel on Christmas Eve, courtesy of Coconut Mushroom – just back from Sweden and No. 3 in the German charts! Far more British and stiff-upper-lip was the 15-shilling Christmas Novelty Dance at Bisley Camp Pavilion, with the pukkah Danny Beaumont Band.

Top dinner dance was the Boxing Night Carnival in the thirteenth-century crypt of the Angel at Guildford, with a five-course meal at 2½ guineas. This is one of those say-it-quick sums of money, since when you sit down to work it out it comes to a massive £2 12*s* 6*d*. As for pantos, who could want more than Bob and Alf Pearson at Camberley Civic Hall? Nothing too Swinging Sixties about that.

In the following week's *Surrey Advertiser*, of 27 December, there was the usual roll call of Christmas casualties, with all figures rising steeply over the previous years. There had been thirty-four accidents (compared with seventeen), four serious casualties (two) and forty-two people slightly hurt (thirteen). A nurse from Egham had been killed.

The Sovereign's Parade at Sandhurst had seen the King and Queen of Tonga and Mrs Kenneth Kaunda, wife of the first Zambian president, among the proud parents watching their sons march out. And more good news came with Guildford Rural Council's announcement that all their houses would be fitted with aerials to pick up 625-line colour transmissions.

At the Yvonne Arnaud Theatre, John Dalby was the writer and star of *The Magic Carpet*, a bright and breezy musical. Second on the bill was David Essex. It would be almost another five years before he found himself in the Top Ten for the first time with 'Rock On' – but by then his Top of the Pops appearances were beaming in on rural Guildford's council houses loud, clear, and more colourful than you could ever have imagined back in '68.

Mrs Stroud's Fund

Back in the 1920s unemployed families in Farnham had their Christmases brightened considerably by a gift fund started in 1922 by Councillor Gertrude Stroud. In his book *Farnham in War and Peace*, published by Phillimore in 1983, W. Ewbank-Smith records that a sum of £118 16*s* was collected in that first year, and vouchers were issued to some 150 households. They were worth between 7*s* 6*d* and 25*s*, according to the number of children in the house aged under fourteen, and with them you could buy meat, groceries or coal. It was certainly popular in those early years, for some 200 families benefited two years later, in 1924. Rather higher up the social register, the Bush Hotel in Farnham revived an old custom by putting a boar's head on the sideboard, writes Mr Ewbank-Smith. 'Visitors were invited to cut themselves a slice, and in the evening the company danced to the music of Cyril Fisher's band.'

The Farnham historian records, however, that more earnest matters were soon concerning the town in the last days of 1924 and the first of the following year. On 28 December the river overflowed into the low-lying streets around, and poured into the basements of several cottages. 'Not since February 1900 has Farnham experienced such a flood as that which covered Bridge Square, Longbridge, Union Road, Lower Church Lane, Vicarage Lane and Downing Street on Friday and Saturday in last week,' the *Farnham Herald* declared on 10 January 1925.

Mr Ewbank-Smith says that the water rose 14 inches in

ground floor rooms in Lower Church Lane. In Vicarage Lane it was lapping up around the fourth stair. There was even a tragedy talked about for years to come, when a big carthorse pulling a vehicle for Beale's the corn merchants slipped and fell: 'They held its head above water until, in the end, they were obliged to shoot the poor beast.' Farnham floods go back centuries, but this start to 1925 was as miserable as many could remember.

Cobbett, Farnham Boy

William Cobbett, journalist, farmer and social reformer, was born in Farnham in 1763 and died close to the town, after the most eventful life imaginable, in 1835. He was the son of a yeoman farmer who also kept a small inn, the Jolly Farmer, on the edge of Farnham, and while Cobbett senior taught the lad the three Rs on dark winter nights, most of young William's memories of his Surrey childhood were of driving a plough for twopence a day, lifting turnips, scaring birds, hoeing peas, weeding the paths at Farnham Castle or leading the horse that pulled the harrow. At fourteen he walked to Kew to see the garden, at nineteen he had run away to London.

But in a lifetime that saw him serve in the army in New Brunswick – having thought he was joining the marines –

William Cobbett, Surrey's social revolutionary.

and living in France and the United States, his tracks finally led back to England and a life that combined publishing in London with farming at some distance from the capital. His best known acres were at Botley, Hampshire, but he also started a farm at Barn Elms, Surrey, and later leased Normandy Farm near Farnham. It was there that he died.

His radical beliefs are best remembered today through the *Rural Rides* which he undertook and reported upon in the later years of his life, from 1821 to 1832. During these years, too, came *A History of the Protestant Reformation*, which is said to have made a mark on such diverse thinkers as Disraeli, Karl Marx, William Morris, Hilaire Belloc and G.K. Chesterton.

The plight of the agricultural poor was never far from Cobbett's thoughts, which makes the Christmas 1829 cartoon seen here, by William Heath, particularly apt. It would be pleasing to

The poor farmer's lot in 1829.

say that there was a Christmas reflection in the *Rural Rides* to complement this drawing, but it is not to be. For a start, the great majority of the rides were undertaken in summer, for obvious reasons. And when we do find Cobbett writing on Christmas Eve, in 1821, his thoughts were alas too full of the practicalities of life for any festive spirit to enter into his journal:

Kensington, Monday, 24 December

> Went from Bergh Apton to Norwich in the morning, and from Norwich to London during the day, carrying with me great admiration of, and respect for, this county of excellent farmers, and hearty, open and spirited men. The Norfolk people are quick and smart in their motions and in their speaking. Very neat and trim in all their farming concerns, and very skilful. Their land is good, their roads are level, and the bottom of their soil is dry, to be sure; and these are great advantages; but they are diligent, and make the most of everything. Their management of all sorts of stock is judicious; they are careful about manure; their teams move quickly; and, in short, it is a county of most excellent cultivators.

Nothing very festive about that late-night thought for Christmas Eve, and when a few days later, on January 2, he travelled through Surrey and Kent to an agricultural debate in Sussex, his mind was still on the diligent East Anglians. 'From the Surrey Wen (city suburbs) to Bromley, the land is generally a deep loam on a gravel', he reports, 'and you see few trees except elm. The agricultural state of the country, or rather the quality of the land, from Bromley to Battle, may be judged of from the fact that I did not see, as I came along, more than 30 acres of swedes during the 56 miles! In Norfolk I should, in the same distance, have seen 500 acres!'

Acknowledgements

All unattributed sections are by the compiler, using printed or original research material. The sources of the other sections are as follows, by permission of or with acknowledgements to the copyright holders:

Bettesworth's Christmas, from *The Bettesworth Book* by George Sturt, alias Bourne, pub. Lamley, 1901; The Singing Men, from *A Walk Through Surrey* by John Moore, pub. Chapman and Hall, 1939; Lighting the Dorking Lamps, Christmas in Old Dorking and Old Christmas Day, from *Recollections of Old Dorking* by Charles Rose, West Surrey Times, 1878; Christmas Stocking, from *Fragments* by Janet Hills, pub. Harold, Margaret and Clare Hills, 1956; Short Truce in a Desperate Christmas, from *Surrey at War* by Bob Ogley, pub. Froglets Publications, 1995; Wassailing the Apple Tree, from *Bygone Haslemere* by E.W. Swanton, pub. West, Newman & Co, London, 1914; Spirited Little Girl, from *Surrey Ghosts Old and New* by Frances D. Stewart, pub. AMCD (publishers) Ltd, 1990; Living Memories, from *Surrey Within Living Memory*, pub. Countryside Books, Newbury and the Surrey Federation of Women's Institutes, Guildford, 1992; Boxing Day Blizzard and The Great Blizzard, January 1881, from *The Surrey Weather Book* by Mark Davison and Ian Currie, pub. Frosted Earth, 1990, reissued 1996; Noel, from *Puttenham People, Tales from a Surrey Village* by Jock Vevers, pub. Screentype 1991, London, 1991; Going Without Help, from *Memoirs of a Surrey Labourer* by George Sturt, alias Bourne, pub. Duckworth, 1907; Recipes from Mrs Beeton's

Book, from *Beeton's Book of Household Management*, by Isabella Beeton, pub. S.O. Beeton, London, 1861; The Christmas Present, from *Sunlight and Shadows* by Charles Kohler, pub. 1974; Reason to Believe, from *Childhood in Edwardian Sussex* by Margaret Hutchinson, pub. Saiga Publishing Co. Ltd, Hindhead, 1981; *In Drear Nighted December* by John Keats, with acknowledgements to Oxford University Press; Never the Same Again and An Inner Beauty, from the *Journals of George Sturt*, ed. D. Mackerness, pub. Cambridge University Press, 1967; December in Richmond Park, from *Round the Year in Richmond Park* by H.R. Hall, pub. Selwyn and Blount, 1923; The Very Best Shop You Know, from *Pot-Pourri from a Surrey Garden* by Mrs C.W. Earle, pub. Smith, Elder, London, 1898; Wraiths at The Rectory, from *Around Haunted Croydon* by Frances D. Stewart, AMCD (publishers) Ltd and Croydon Libraries, 1989; Mrs Stroud's Fund, a précis of material in *Farnham in War and Peace* by W. Ewbank-Smith, pub. Phillimore, 1983.

Thanks are due to the staffs of the local studies centres at Richmond and Guildford Libraries; and especially, for help in production, to Jane Calvert of France Lynch, near Stroud.

Picture Credits

Pictures are from the compiler's collection except various press cuttings and page 2, top, *Illustrated London News*; pages 5, 26, 49, 75, 93, 98, 103, 106, Wigan Heritage Service; page 47, Lancashire County Libraries.